"Few people have done more to inspire an entrepreneur revolution and give entrepreneurs the tools and advice they need to grow their businesses in recent years than Dan. What I love about what he says and what he writes is that it all comes from a deep personal experience of bootstrapping a successful global small business himself from little more than a maxed out credit card."

Mike Harris, Founder of FirstDirect and Egg PLC,
Author of *Find Your Lightbulb*

"We live in the Age of the Entrepreneur, surrounded by some tremendously innovative, fast-growing and game-changing companies. By nature, entrepreneurs are always looking forward and identifying new opportunities. However, the truly great entrepreneurs also use lessons from past successes and failures and learn from those who have gone before them. Daniel's book is a brilliant resource to help entrepreneurs 'find their place' and live the 'entrepreneur revolution dream.'"

Alistair Lukies, CEO of Monitise and cited by David
Cameron as one of Britain's most inspiring entrepreneurs

"Daniel Priestley's book *Entrepreneur Revolution* perfectly teaches how to adopt an enterprising, street-smart mindset that produces results. His own failures, like mine, have taught him valuable and practical down-to earth lessons which any aspiring leaders can learn from and will enjoy trying and applying themselves."

Lara Morgan, Founder of Pacific Direct

"Daniel Priestley will help anyone with the drive and determination to start their own business (or explode an existing one), so that they can transform their lives, improve their finances radically and raise their quality of life substantially. Not only does Daniel walk the talk of the Entrepreneur Revolution, but he has inspired thousands of others to do the same. I know, like and trust this man, and follow his wisdom. If you want to play a bigger part in the Entrepreneur Revolution and you have any sense whatsoever, then you'll do the same."

Steve Bolton, Founder, Platinum Property Partners,
President of Peace One Day Patrons and Author of
***Successful Property Investing* and other books**

"Daniel Priestly is one of a kind. Having worked with him for many years now, I can clearly see his unique ability to intuitively identify a collective need and provide a completely innovative solution, always at the right time and in the right place. He truly is an extraordinary individual and a phenomenon in the entrepreneurial world."

Andrew Griffiths, Australia's #1 Small Business Author

"Most entrepreneurs have been through some sort of a shift due to the recent economic correction. Some fell by the wayside gave up their dreams and went back into the workforce to be safe. Other entrepreneurs stepped up and said 'now is my time to shine while the economy is down'. Daniel is the modern day entrepreneur and is certainly one that has stepped up to create an amazing infrastructure to enable entrepreneurs to take their business to the next level. You probably have lots of books you want to read to help you grow your business: put this on top of the pile."

Anthony Amos, Founder of HydroDog

"Daniel Priestley's book will help any entrepreneur focus on building a huge business in a controlled, focused fashion. Daniel's book gives you a blueprint for success!"

Kevin Harrington, Founder and Chairman of
As Seen on TV Inc, and "Shark" for three seasons on
the ABC Network hit show *Shark Tank*

"Building a business requires both aspiration and inspiration. *Entrepreneur Revolution* delivers on both."

Guy Rigby, Partner, Head of Entrepreneurs,
Smith & Williamson LLP and Author of *From Vision to Exit*

"Daniel's writing helps business owners realize that they are an expert in their chosen field, that they are sitting on a mountain of value and they have the opportunity to influence the world just by being themselves and bringing their best to the table every time they do business. It's inspiring, simple and incredibly effective stuff."

David Hooton, Founder of Platform Networks,
Australia, www.hooton.org

"Daniel's analysis of where we stand – on the brink of a global, small business revolution – is startling. If he's right, he's 20 years ahead of the game and we need to be taking action now. Who's ready to sail on the crest of the seismic wave that will ultimately change the way we all work forever? It's not sink or swim time yet, but it is the moment to get miles out in front of the competition. You can start building the ark that will weather the storms of tomorrow and leave you smiling, fulfilled and richly rewarded. Daniel can show you the entrepreneur's essential mindset and the secrets of tapping into the power of a technological revolution which is only just beginning."

Oliver Selway, Personal Trainer, Founder of Paleo Training, UK

"Daniel Priestley has totally revolutionized my thinking. I have emerged from being a factory worker with a monkey brain to an entrepreneur. My entire life has changed and I am finally in a position to make a difference to those around me. Thank you Daniel."

Sonya Blondinau, Executive Coach, Founder of Walk Like a Rock Star

"*Entrepreneur Revolution* is a must-read for anyone wanting to leave their treadmill job behind and join the movement of global small businesses. Daniel's experience in helping small business owners become great is invaluable and this book holds all his gems in an easy-to-read, easy-to-understand and comprehensive form. If you want to join the entrepreneur revolution – buy this book – highly recommended."

Jessica McGregor Johnson, International Speaker and Coach and Author of *The Right T-Shirt: Write Your Own Rules and Live the Life You Want*

"Technology will speed a change in our thinking, access to opportunities and personal desire for success over the coming years in a way we can only imagine. Daniel Priestley's book *Entrepreneur Revolution* lays out the 10 challenges facing us and gives us the opportunity to get on board … Unless you are happy to sit in the station watching everything pass you by … Read this book now … twice!"

Vicki Wusche, Founder of The Property Mermaid, www.vickiwusche.com

"Having read Daniel's first book *Key Person of Influence*, I really couldn't wait to read his new title *Entrepreneur Revolution*. I must say that it certainly didn't disappoint! In his new book, Daniel shares some incredible insights into how modern technology is set to change the business landscape over the coming decades. Truly thought-provoking, and an absolute must-read for business owners and entrepreneurs who are serious about staying ahead of the game."

Matt Gubba, British Entrepreneur and Founder of Business Circuit

"Daniel's actually implemented everything he talks and writes about and can speak with authority about what works and what doesn't. I have recommended to many of my friends and colleagues that they engage in the Key Person of Influence Program and would say to anyone who is contemplating making their mark on the world: Read This Book!"

Ned Coten, MD of Acorn Brand Design

"When I started out in business, entrepreneurs were considered weird people who dropped out of school and couldn't get a job. As Daniel has shown, now is the rise of entrepreneurship as a vehicle for highly talented and skilled people to build something that gives them a better life than a boring corporate job. This book will totally change the way you think about growing a business. An absolute must read that should be in the hands of more people."

Jeremy Harbour, Author of *Go Do!*, Founder of The Unity Group

ENTREPRENEUR REVOLUTION

How to develop your entrepreneurial mindset and start a business that works

Daniel Priestley

CAPSTONE

A catalogue record for this book is available from the Library of Congress
A catalogue record for this book is available from the British Library

ISBN 978-0-857-08416-3 (paperback) ISBN 978-0-857-08413-2 (ebk)
ISBN 978-0-857-08414-9 (ebk) ISBN 978-0-857-08415-6 (ebk)

Cover design: Parent Design Ltd
Set in 11/16pt Adobe Jenson Pro by Sparks – www.sparkspublishing.com
Printed in Great Britain by TJ International Ltd, Padstow, Cornwall, UK

CONTENTS

DEDICATION

This book is dedicated to the bravest, most authentic, creative, expansive, dynamic people I know: the entrepreneurs of the world.

To the farmer I met in Uganda who had the courage to take a micro-loan and lift herself from poverty through her chicken business.

To the IT manager who dared to pitch an "impossible idea" to the chairman of his bank and created three iconic businesses, and has helped hundreds of entrepreneurs and became the best mentor I could have dreamed of.

To the 16 year old who started *Student* magazine and ended up inspiring a generation of entrepreneurs.

To the 30 year old who was fired from his own technology company for being too disruptive, only to save the company ten years later by revolutionizing every industry he touched. True icons leave early – we will miss him.

To the person who bit the bullet today and registered their first business.

This book is my tribute to you. I'm just as excited as you are!

INTRODUCTION

The idea of the Entrepreneur Revolution is that the rules that created commercial success in the past have radically changed. Doing what worked yesterday may not bring you success tomorrow.

For some people, this will be a time of great uncertainty and loss. For others it will be the greatest opportunity in history.

An entrepreneur is simply someone who spots an opportunity and acts to make it into a commercial success.

This book is written to help *you* to become better at spotting opportunities and turning them into a commercial success.

A revolution is a great shift in society, where an old system is thrown out and a new one is embraced. In all of history, the real fortunes are made in revolutionary times. The difference with this revolution is that it presents a chance for wealth to spread to a lot more people. The tools, technology and opportunities that have shown up recently are designed to empower people. Lots of people.

Today, farmers in rural India have access to more computing power than NASA had when it launched *Apollo 11*.

Today, a teenager in their bedroom has more tools for building a global enterprise than Coca-Cola did when it grew internationally.

Today, your business ideas have more potential to be massive than ever before in history.

For whatever reason, you were born to live through these exciting times. You weren't born to live in the dark ages as a serf, you weren't born to live in the agricultural ages as a farmer, you weren't born to live in the industrial age as a factory worker. You are alive during a unique point in history; a time where anything is possible for you.

This book is here to wake up the part of you that can spot opportunities and make them successful. Not just any opportunities, but those that are right for you.

In these pages you will discover that there's a part of your brain that is already highly entrepreneurial and wants to build something you can be proud of. You'll discover exactly how to live in the "entrepreneur sweet spot" where you do what you love, you do it well and you get rewarded generously for it.

This book will challenge you too. I've laid out ten challenges for you to get started on almost immediately. They are designed to push your buttons and get you out of your comfort zone.

I'll give you a way of creating a high-performance culture, so that no matter how many complex decisions you face, you will always continue to move forward.

I've also hidden a few little gems in this book – ideas that I refer to, but don't specifically reveal in black and white.

There's an underlying theme, relating to a key ingredient, that you need if you really want to be successful. You might spot it straight away, or it might come to you later.

YOU MIGHT WANT TO READ THIS BOOK MORE THAN ONCE

If you do spot the new ingredient, pay particular attention to put it into everything you do. This new ingredient hasn't been necessary in business up until this point but, from now on, it must be at the very heart of what you do.

I'm going to mention this ingredient many times in the book, but I won't say what it is specifically for you. I will leave you to find it.

When you read through this book, look for this magic ingredient, or at least look for clues.

The beginning is important and the end will unfold but, at the centre, you might discover a mountain of value you never noticed when you first looked.

Sometimes people read this book and "get it" – other times they don't. Some people get it on the second or third read. I've not hidden this key ingredient from you; if anything it's actually right under your nose.

Whatever you do, don't stop looking. You simply can't build a successful enterprise without this ingredient in the Entrepreneur Revolution.

Good luck. I hope you love reading this book.

To keep in touch with the author visit:

www.entrevo.com/danielpriestley

PART I

BREAKING FREE FROM THE INDUSTRIAL REVOLUTION ECONOMY

CHAPTER 1

THE ENTREPRENEUR REVOLUTION IS HAPPENING

The word "revolution" gets bandied about an awful lot. I've heard soft drinks being described as "a revolution." I've seen car commercials portraying their latest model as "revolutionary."

So I forgive you if you rolled your eyes when you read the title of this book for the first time.

I want you to know, however, that I haven't used the word lightly. I use the word "revolution" with all the gravity and reverence that I can muster.

What's about to take place is a revolution. Everything as you know it will change in the coming years.

The nature of work, lifestyle and wealth is all about to change.

Before we look forward, however, let's look backwards at the last revolution.

Let's begin at the agricultural age. If you went back 250 years in a time machine, the chances are the first person you would meet would be a farmer. The agricultural age was defined by the fact that most people worked the land.

Then came a technological breakthrough. The steam engine, fossil fuels and machinery.

One tractor could do the work of 100 men in the field. One textile factory could make all the suits for a city at a fraction of the cost of a tailor.

The technology changed things. You couldn't fight it, you couldn't avoid it, it was a revolution.

If you took your time machine back any time between about 1850 and the year 2000, there's a lot less chance you would meet a single farmer, even if you tried. You would meet factory workers.

In the early part of the revolution, you would see people who worked on machines making products. They were "blue collar" factory workers. If you went back to the late 1900s you would find people working on the new machines – computers – making data. These were "white collar" factory workers.

Regardless of the colour of their collar, their labour is repetitive. They sit at their work station and they repeat their tasks for hours on end until the day is over. This is just how it is for most people who live in the industrial age.

I believe that we are at the dawn of a new age. We are leaving the Industrial Revolution and we are entering the "Entrepreneur Revolution."

This means, quite simply, if you took your time machine forward to any time in the next 100 years you would most likely meet people who work in small businesses in an "entrepreneurial team."

Why do I believe this?

Once again, it's technology that has changed things. It's technology that has robbed the big factories of their awesome competitive advantage and given an edge to small businesses.

Technology has made it possible for any small business to find a market globally, to access factories, to build a brand, to be open for business 24/7 and to innovate.

Small businesses can do almost all the things big businesses can do; and they can do something more.

A small business has spirit. It has a team of people who care, they know their customers, they love what they do, they respond faster, there's less red tape, the workplace is more fun and everyone gets to have a say.

SMALL BUSINESSES CAN MAKE A DIFFERENCE

When a company has less than 150 staff, everyone tends to know everyone else. There's a buzz and an excitement. There's a tribal feeling that often gets lost in big corporations.

When the founder of the business is involved in the operations, there's magic. Rarely is this magic scalable for big business.

For these reasons and more, top performers are going to quit their jobs and start businesses. They are going to take with them the other top performers.

These entrepreneurial teams will be faster, more cost effective, more nimble, more responsive and more profitable.

So, if the technology has created a revolution, let's take a quick look at how this revolution got started and when it's likely to take off.

In the late 1800s the telephone was invented, but it wasn't until the 1920s that it took off. It made it feasible for businesses to have multiple local locations.

In the 1920s commercial air travel was born, but it wasn't until the 1950s that it was popularized. Once again, a 20–30 year lag time before the systemic changes arrived. Once air travel was widely available, we saw the birth of national and international companies.

In the 1930s, along came TV. However, most people believe it was a 1950s phenomenon; again a 20-year lag time. Television gave birth to the brand. Whoever dominated the airwaves dominated people's spending habits.

Jump forward to the late 1960s and you will see the first computers. It wasn't until the 1980s, however, that computers were being purchased by a significant number of businesses or individuals.

You might not have spotted it right away but, if you looked closely, in the 1980s and 1990s people were beginning to use their computers in home-based business.

These home-based businesses might have been tiny, but they didn't necessarily appear so. For the first time in over 100 years, small businesses could be just as competitive as large businesses.

In 1989, Tim Berners-Lee came up with the world wide web and the internet was born. Again, it took close to 20 years for the majority to adopt it, and I was surprised to discover that, even in 2010, over 20% of people in the UK still didn't have broadband internet connection at home.

In 1998, Google made the whole web searchable. Anything you want, anyone you need, any question you have, all discovered in a matter of seconds.

In 2004, social media was born, democratizing information in a way that enabled people who shared common interests to find each other and share ideas as never before.

In 2008, cloud computing was born, giving rise to the "virtual business." Staff and customers can be anywhere in the world and the business is exactly the same. Work can be done from home, teams can be spaced out globally and no one cares.

Twenty to thirty years. That's the lag time for business to really catch on.

We're just seeing the effects of the internet in 2010. We'll probably see the true effects of Google around 2020, and the impact of the social web and cloud computing in 2030 and beyond.

We don't need to wait though; we know what's going to happen.

All of this technology can make a small business look big. It makes micro-niches accessible. It levels the playing field.

So, let's be honest. Where would you rather work? Would you like to work in a soulless company that cares only about its balance sheet and treats you like a number? Or, instead, would you like to be part of a small, dynamic team of creative people who are servicing the needs of a niche you feel passionate about?

An entrepreneur is not just the founder of the business. In my opinion, founders get too much credit. An entrepreneur is someone who makes valuable things happen and who takes full responsibility for their success or failure.

In that context, high-performing entrepreneurial teams can only exist because the "entrepreneurship" is shared by the leaders, managers and team members and not just the person who started the business entity.

Your goal in the Entrepreneur Revolution is to create value, to take on meaningful work and to care deeply about what you are involved in.

Would you like to work for a company that says "we can't spend shareholders' money on community projects and we can't waste money on buying ethically produced inputs"?

Or would you like to work for a company that says, "We care. End of story. If we can make a positive impact, it's more important than squeezing out every last cent of profit."

Chances are, if you are a top performer, you want to work somewhere that you are recognized and where you feel that the work you do makes a difference.

If you're an entrepreneur, then this is your time. Never in history has there been a better time for you to start and grow a business, that brings excitement to the workplace and makes an inspiring difference to the world.

And so the Entrepreneur Revolution will take place. There's no point fighting it. It's happening.

This book is designed to help you to transition out of the old and into the new. It's designed to get you ahead of the curve, seeing the future and making the most of it.

Just like the farmers had to change the way they viewed the world or they would end up as factory fodder, we too must change. We must develop a more entrepreneurial nature.

We must wake up the part of ourselves that is OK with change, that loves a challenge, that takes responsibility and that cares.

We must cease being "factory workers" and start being entrepreneurs.

To see Daniel talk about the Entrepreneur Revolution visit:
www.entrevo.com/talk-er

CHAPTER 2

THE RISE OF THE GLOBAL SMALL BUSINESS

Not too long from now, almost every business will be a multinational. Tiny little businesses will behave big. There will be millions of "global small businesses."

The global small business (GSB) isn't like a big global business, and neither is it like a traditional small business. As the name suggests, this is a business that typically has less than 20 staff but isn't limited by geography. It can reach into cities all over the world and can easily be making millions in sales despite a relatively small headcount.

Most commonly, GSBs will be service providers, or offer intangible products like software and information. However, many will also sell high-value physical products that can be sent whizzing all over the globe to customers in faraway cities.

A lot of GSBs will also have valuable intellectual property that they license to their "local partners."

Global small businesses will have incredibly well developed brands compared to traditional small businesses, making them look much bigger than they are. It will be clear what these businesses value; their "look and feel" will be consistent across several social media platforms.

They will be built around a "micro-niche." Rather than being a business for "health and wellness" they will be for "vegetarian marathon runners" or "triathlon mums."

A GSB can function in the tiniest of niches and go miles deep with its clients (or its "tribe," as author, Seth Godin would say).

GSBs will be great with digital media. They will interact with the world through video on the web, articles, audio podcasts, downloads, streaming live events, slideshows, blogs, tweets and communities.

A GSB will revolve around the special talents of a few key people of influence. The business will outsource almost every function that is not clearly creating value.

Inside the team will be communications experts and product designers. The one common thread is that you MUST share the passion of the business if you want to be on the team.

These GSB teams might not be in the same geographical location. They will communicate on instant messaging platforms, market themselves using social media, manage their operations in the cloud and be based wherever it makes sense from a tax and IP protection standpoint (I predict Singapore and Luxembourg being front runners).

The GSBs will have their top talent working from home offices and meeting in rented boardrooms on a weekly or monthly basis. Due to multiple time zones the edges of work and play will blur. Performance will be more important than hours clocked – "the only truth is the results" is the new mantra for managing employees of GSBs.

GSBs will become an attractive alternative to white collar employment. Professionals like lawyers, accountants, consultants and managers will define a micro-niche and then leave traditional employment in favour of their own GSB start-up, or join a GSB that stirs up their underlying passion.

Lifestyle and flexibility will be a huge advantage for a GSB. Correctly structured, the owners of GSBs will pay little tax compared to their employee counterparts. Many

GSB owners will split their time living in 2–3 locations to avoid income tax altogether.

Having a GSB will create an enviable lifestyle. A GSB isn't like having a traditional, local small business that prevents the owner from travelling and limits the money they can make to the local economy.

A GSB, on the contrary, *expands* as you travel and is only limited by the size of the micro-niche and the creativity of the team. Many GSBs will earn millions in revenue and have only a few staff (some of whom will be based in low-labour-cost countries like the Philippines, India or Thailand). For this reason, many GSB owners will earn seven-figure salaries with comparative ease.

The GSB is an exciting new category of business to look out for in the decade ahead as the barriers to entry drop for doing business across borders.

Your next project might be for a GSB. You might even be setting up one for yourself.

There's a good chance, if you're reading a book like this, that I may bump into you a few years from now and you will be living fully in the Entrepreneur Revolution enjoying the benefits of your GSB.

You'll have the power to log into your business from your smartphone anywhere in the world. You will be able to see sales figures, workflow and financials instantly.

You will probably have a company based in a low tax environment but have customers all over the world. You will probably spend a lot of your time travelling around on a working holiday.

Your business won't sleep. You'll be making money 24/7 and you'll have clients in time zones that wrap around the world.

All of this is made possible by the times we are in. The foundations have been laid for people like yourself to unfold your passion into a highly functional business that delivers a ton of value to the world.

IT'S TIME TO CHOOSE

It sounds idealistic. However, it's entirely realistic. These are the times we live in. You have the power and the choice to leave the Industrial Revolution model of employment and step into an age of empowerment and enterprise.

For the next 50 years, the two systems will still co-exist side by side and it will be your choice which one you want to operate in.

Already I attend dinner parties with both groups of people. On one side of the table are my friends working in corporations (white collar factories). They steer the conversation towards issues of job security and retirement. They complain that they aren't fulfilled in their work, they find it hard to move up the ladder and they aren't able to save enough money for the holidays, retirement and lifestyle they want.

On the other side of the table are my entrepreneurial friends. Times are good for them and getting better. They talk about their latest product launch, their new technology and the freedom it's brought them. They are in control of their destiny and feel fulfilled in life. Also, they have discovered that they can make exponentially more money in their own business than in a job, and they don't ever feel the need to retire.

The Industrial Revolution model is a slowly dying animal. It's fundamentally not right for the times we live in. The entrepreneurial GSB is nimble, dynamic and rewarding.

The choice is in your hands. Do you want to let go fully of the past and embrace these revolutionary times we are in, or do you want to try to do things the way they've always been done?

NOW IS THE TIME TO CHOOSE

Right now, we are at a cusp in history. It's a revolutionary time.

Technology, since the year 2000, has been building and building like a giant wave. This wave has grown in size and speed thanks to something called "convergence."

Convergence is when several unrelated ideas bump into each other and create massive, unpredictable results.

Digital cameras meet mobile phones and create camera phones. Camera phones meet social networking and, suddenly, news breaks on Twitter rather than on CNN.

Touch screens meet ultra-thin lithium batteries and iPads are born. iPads meet digital book libraries and the publishing industry radically shifts.

Google Maps bumps into precise sensor technology, packaged inside electric cars, and suddenly vehicles don't need human drivers.

Huge breakthrough technologies are all bumping into each other. Smartphones, cloud computing, voice recognition, social influence, collaborative workspace, tablet PCs, cheap travel, resource capacity sharing, free video conferencing, RDF chips, emerging middle class consumers in Asia, crowdfunding, automation, robots, DNA sequencing, 3D printing, self-checkout, intuitive user experience, automated intelligence, gesture recognition, open source operating systems, multi-device ecosystems, face recognition ... and the list goes on and on.

Each of these ideas, on its own, has the power to shift industries; but it's bigger than that. These technologies are all bumping into each other!

A great wave of change is about to seriously take off and a wedge will be driven between two classes of people.

1. Those who are surfing this wave into the Entrepreneur Revolution.
2. Those who are clinging to the Industrial Revolution and are in serious trouble whether they know it or not.

The surfers are the ones who embrace change, are future focused and who have positioned themselves to catch the wave and have fun with it.

Those who are in trouble are unaware of what's happening, happily clinging to old ways of doing things, expecting their future to be much the same as the past.

As dramatic as it sounds, I genuinely believe there's now just a brief window of time for people to "get with the programme" or risk getting left behind.

If you're reading this book, I dare say you're at the very least curious about stepping away from the old paradigms and towards the new.

If so, let's begin to take some steps forward into the Entrepreneur Revolution. If you're ready, turn the page and let's begin the journey.

CHAPTER 3

LET'S LOOK AT THE SYSTEM

When I look around, I see people living according to a system that makes very little sense to me anymore.

I see people giving up the best part of their day, to push power to a vision that doesn't inspire them, for a small amount of money that barely affords them an exciting life.

I see people who are stuck with mortgages that limit every decision they make. People who live in towns that they chose because they grew up there (but never looked anywhere else).

I notice some people who have friends they don't respect or admire. They are friends just because they have always been friends.

I see people who hold ideas, religious or otherwise, that don't really make a lot of sense to them but they believe because everyone else does.

So many people are living by their past decisions. Or, even worse, they are living by someone else's past decisions.

Over the last 150 years that hasn't been such a bad thing. The Industrial Revolution set the tone; working for a factory or a big corporation was the norm. As a worker you needed to be on site every day from 8:30am to 5:30pm, travel was something you had to squeeze into your annual leave, fun was something you could look forward to when you were too old for it.

The Industrial Revolution caused a massive shift in the way we live. Prior to this factory age, we were all entrepreneurs. We were butchers, bakers and candlestick makers. We knew the names of our customers, people knew our names (in fact they made our names from our little businesses – Robert Butcher, John Baker, Sally Candlestickmaker).

Then, along came the machines. Steam engines, cars, sewing machines, tractors and the like. Forward thinking people, who could afford to buy machines, multiplied their wealth and made vast fortunes. Those who didn't have the means were swept up onto the factory floor to become faceless, nameless corporate slaves.

Once again the world is changing. The internet changes everything. It gives everyone new powers to create from anywhere in the world. It gives you a TV station for free, a radio station for free, a daily publication for free and a way of selling products and services for free. It takes your ideas and products and distributes them for you globally.

It allows you to make money from tiny, silly little ideas.

Radically, it allows people to make money from their passion. An idea that seems so foreign to so many.

What is to come will be called the "Entrepreneur Revolution" many years from now.

This is a new age, where people are free to earn while they explore. Their personal breakthroughs, their journey of self-discovery and their expression of creativity will replace the daily grind of the workplace.

At the beginning of the Industrial Revolution a factory cost a fortune to set up. Now the "factory" costs a few thousand dollars to set up. To be in business today requires you to have a laptop, a phone and an idea.

This simple fact has given birth to a new breed of person: part owner, part worker, part artist. The new breed of entrepreneurs has arrived.

Big companies will find it hard to compete with small ones. Small companies will reinvent themselves almost every year or two. People will matter again, causes will matter again and maybe we will see a world that works for a lot more people.

For me, this has been a discovery I have witnessed first-hand.

I am an entrepreneur. In fact, I've never had a traditional job with a secure annual wage in my life.

I grew up in a beachside town in Australia. As a teenager I worked at McDonald's, I delivered pizza, I went door-to-door selling and I worked behind a bar.

All through my teen years I wanted to be an entrepreneur. I read books about business, I read business magazines and I collected articles about entrepreneurs who had been successful.

At 19 I went to university to study business. I believed that I would be rubbing shoulders with multi-millionaire entrepreneurs and learning about how to raise big money, grow fast and exit big.

I was disappointed at university. None of my lecturers had built or sold businesses. Most of them were struggling. At age 20, I dropped out of university to work directly for a successful entrepreneur. I shadowed him for almost two years. I learned all about sales, marketing, product creation, team building and managing fast growth. It was exactly the kind of learning I had wanted from university!

I founded my first company at 22 years old after two years of apprenticeship in a fast-growth marketing business.

I created a highly niched marketing business specializing in event marketing and sales follow-up. By 25, I had a team of over 15 people and we were generating millions in sales.

At 25, I decided to expand internationally and set up an office in London. We generated millions in sales in the first year despite being warned that London was a tough city.

In my late 20s, business took me all over the world. I visited dozens of countries, did deals, worked alongside some awe-inspiring entrepreneurs and rubbed shoulders with my childhood heroes.

At age 29, I wrote a book called *Key Person of Influence*. It became a business best-seller and it put me in contact with thousands of entrepreneurs.

As a result, we set up a business growth accelerator specializing in small service businesses. Within three years we were set up in multiple countries, helping hundreds of entrepreneurs to grow their businesses with support from some of the world's most successful business leaders who are part of the programme. Without a doubt, it's been an exciting journey thus far.

Along the way, I have set up side ventures, I've bought and sold businesses and I've raised money and invested in all sorts of enterprises. I've also used my businesses to raise hundreds of thousands of dollars for charities.

I've had some stunning wins and some cringeworthy flops (I've learned more from the flops than the wins). I've formed some deep friendships through the extreme ups and downs. I've also had some intense fights.

I've witnessed a huge shift in the way business is done in just ten years. From what I've witnessed first-hand, I feel very strongly that the world is going through a radical transformation.

Had I been slightly older, I would have been more established when the internet came along and I might have missed out on being part of the digital trends over the last ten years. I wouldn't have paid enough attention to the radical shifts that the internet has caused.

Had I been much younger, I would have started in business focused only on digital trends. I wouldn't have seen the big shifts because I wouldn't have had any grounding in traditional business.

As it happened, I got into business at the right age and the right time to witness a radical shift. It's an incredible shift that I refer to as the "Entrepreneur Revolution."

Today I live the Entrepreneur Revolution lifestyle. I travel the world, I earn money from my global small businesses, my time is my own, I raise money for causes that matter to me and I feel a huge sense of freedom.

When I want to take a break I can, when I want to attend an exciting event I do, if I want to buy something special I don't need to think about the money.

Better still, almost every day I get emails from clients saying they love working with us, they want to recommend us and they feel we've made a difference to them.

I have an awesome team. My business partners are my closest friends, we have incredibly talented people who have been proudly creating with us for years. We have charity partners who are now expanding their reach as a result of the partnership we have with them.

I'm not saying all that to be boastful, I'm saying it because I feel it has come as a result of being tapped into the Entrepreneur Revolution. As the industrial age comes to an end, the entrepreneurial age is in full swing.

I owe my lifestyle to the new emerging world. I owe it to the internet being everywhere, valuable digital services being cheap or free, the cloud making my enterprise instantly global and living in an age of collaboration.

Everything indicates this isn't a blip on the radar. It's all getting better and easier as I let go fully of the industrialized worker mindset and fully embrace the Entrepreneur Revolution that's taking place.

Living in the Entrepreneur Revolution, it seems perfectly normal to live a life that's very free.

It's a foreign idea to wake up to an alarm, to have a person who I think of as my boss, or to ask permission to get on a plane and go away for a week.

Through the miraculous technology of Facebook, I have kept contact with my friends who haven't busted loose yet; the people who got good grades and then got good jobs. I see that behind the great corporate titles are very boring jobs. Behind the annual holidays are people sitting at their desks most of the year counting down the days until the next break comes around.

It's a choice. Times have changed and we live in a unique time where if you want a steady job you can have one or if you want to make just as much money doing whatever you like, whenever you like, with whoever you like, you can do that too.

It's just as much effort to hold down a good job today as it is to be completely free as a bird. It's just a choice you make. Do you want to live according to the rules of the Industrial Revolution or the Entrepreneur Revolution?

This book is designed for people who want to live by a set of new rules. The Entrepreneur Revolution rules.

If you're still reading, I'm sure you want to fully embrace the time we're in and live by these new rules. However, it's not quite as simple as it sounds.

In the same way that your computer can't function properly without upgrading its software, you must also be willing to delete some old files from your mind and install some new (somewhat radical) ideas.

In the next few chapters we're going to take a critical look at the current system, and I'm going to suggest some ways to break out of it.

When you're ready to shake up your world with some fresh ideas, read over the next few chapters. I will take you on a journey. It's the journey I have been on and I will give you the lessons that I learned along the way.

Some of the lessons you might already agree with. Some may challenge you. Some may give you the key to the lock that opens the door to a whole new way of being – if only you're willing to try them out. Let's take a look.

IT'S A SYSTEM THAT'S NO LONGER RIGHT FOR US

It's time we had a very honest conversation about the industrialized system we have bought into. It's a system that transformed humanity more than any other. As a result of the Industrial Revolution we have better health, more wealth and technology.

The Industrial Revolution is an awe-inspiring time in history. However, I believe it's a system that no longer serves you.

The system is made up of rules and ideas that were perfect for the Industrial Revolution but they are no longer right for people who choose to live in the Entrepreneur Revolution.

The Industrial Revolution needed workers to perform meaningless, repetitive tasks. It needed lots of them.

The Entrepreneur Revolution needs people who are passionate, free thinking, inspired innovators. The systems and rules for creating people like that are different to the rules used to create industrialized workers.

Let's take three simple ideas: ideas that work when applied to the Industrial Revolution but don't serve you in the Entrepreneur Revolution.

1. "Work hard now and you will get your rewards later."
2. "Work isn't meant to be fun."
3. "Do your homework to prove how smart you are."

These are just three examples I use to show how differently you must start to think if you're going to take full advantage of the times we are in.

Just like it was explained in the movie *The Matrix*, the system creeps up on you and it hums along in the background like a motor; most people can't see it, hear it, feel it and they certainly don't think about it.

Let's start with the first simple idea.

OLD IDEA: WORK HARD NOW AND YOU WILL GET YOUR REWARDS LATER

This idea is in religion, in institutional work, in governments, in schools and many other places you look; the idea that you should make sacrifices now for some far-off reward in the future.

It isn't the case. Right here, in this moment, is all your power, all your joy, all your life force. You have no power in the future or in the past, it's all here in this moment.

When you are present to your true feelings, you make better choices. When you project yourself into the future or the past you lose your power.

I'm not talking about people who are following an in-spired path where they love the journey and they also have a big goal in mind (like an Olympic athlete or a start-up business). Even though the rewards are in the future, these people are engaged just as much in their present journey.

When I talk about people who are paralyzed by the "jam tomorrow game," I'm talking about people who are stuck doing something they hate because they think some day it will pay off and the rewards will be worth it.

Agents of the Industrial Revolution controlled workers with the idea that in the future they would have great rewards for their labour if they suffered now. Far too often, people put their real dreams on hold so they can work more for their industrial-age employer.

Here's the newsflash: if you're doing something you hate, I'm here to tell you your sacrifice probably won't deliver a pay-off in the future. You will probably just spend a whole lifetime making sacrifices and then get resentful that you're too old to do the things that really matter to you.

If you continue to sacrifice, you will probably realize after it's too late that a great life is made up of great days.

New Idea: There is no pay day, there's just life

Reading this, you might start to feel annoyed. You might think that sacrificing now for a distant reward is just the way it is and that I am mad for suggesting otherwise.

So, let's question it. Take a look around at those of your friends who are sacrificing now so they can get ahead later. Is it actually paying off for them? Does it matter if they are 30, 40 or 50 years old? Is it working?

What about you? Are you playing the "delayed gratification game" by putting things off for the future, and how is it working out for you?

Surely, if this idea worked, it would be really starting to show signs of producing results by now, right? Surely if you have been putting off big dreams for 15 years there would be some pretty big rewards starting to stack up already ... surely if this idea works you could see the evidence starting to show?

For most people I speak to it hasn't started to show up in a big way ... and if it has, the sacrifice wasn't worth it. They gave up the best part of their 20s and 30s only to spark a reckless midlife crisis later in life.

I have spoken to countless people who get themselves in debt in their 20s, trying to "get ahead" through home ownership. The mortgage was crippling and property didn't perform the way it did for the baby boomers. By the time they get their head back above water, they feel unable to take financial risks ever again and they are very keen to play catch-ups on lost holidays. They end up in a confused state.

When I probe into a person's best choice, more often than not it arose from being brave and seizing the moment. Rarely do people achieve momentous things because they hesitated and put off what their heart was calling them to do.

For me the idea of passing up the most virile, energetic years of my life so I can take a few Euro-getaway tours in my 70s is a complete non-starter. It's crazy! Why play golf when you could have played anything? Why wait until you are too old to do the things you are waiting to do?

Why cash in the nest egg when you could have been free as a bird in the first place?

One reason is fear. We are scared of living in the present because of what might happen in the future.

Ironically, from a place of centredness, here in the present, we have our most authentic and powerful visions for the future.

The place to plan your future is in the present. The best place is on the beach or in a forest or in a rooftop penthouse apartment. If you are inspired you will create an inspired vision. If you are fearful you will create a vision based on mitigating your fear. It will be about scarcity and not abundance.

I'm not saying that you don't have goals, dreams and plans. I'm saying that you are living in a time where they can happen now, not later.

We are stuck with remnants of the industrialized worker mentality. We think it's wrong to have fun all day, it's wasteful to sit and think, it's somehow bad to question authority. All of those ideas were taught to you at school or in your first apprentice programme.

Old Idea: Work isn't meant to be fun

My grandfather worked hard. He was a factory technician making copper cable. It was hard work, in hot tin sheds with loud machines.

My grandfather got injured at work. He almost blinded himself when sparks flew in his face. Another time he chopped off a big chunk of his finger when he was operating heavy machinery. He didn't take time off, he was back at work the next day.

Apparently this was a good thing. It proved how hard he was willing to work and that getting work done was most important.

He got promoted to a junior manager, a foreman, then a middle manager. Eventually he became the general manager of the whole factory.

He never expected that work would be fun, he had his weekends for that. On weekends he liked to play golf or go fishing. Golf and fishing were fun, work was hard. Simple.

New Idea: Fun Builds Your Business

In the Entrepreneur Revolution it doesn't have to be that way. If he were alive today, and so inclined, my grandpa could easily make golf and fishing a business. He could build a website, he could invent products, he could have a community of like-minded people who subscribe to his tips, he could be an affiliate for other great products that he discovers.

Today he could join a team anywhere in the world and work from home. His passion, combined with his methodical approach, could make him invaluable to a Global Small Business.

Today, working hard probably indicates you are doing something functional, not something valuable.

People who thrive in the Entrepreneur Revolution don't work hard. They create, they get stuff done, they make things happen, they organize change, they drive projects, they engineer results.

Sometimes this requires dedicated effort, sometimes it takes time to work the angles, often there's many conversations to be had. However, it's not "work" that is being done. At least not in the traditional sense.

Old Idea: Work Hard To Prove How Smart You Are

One of the first rules you learn in school is that it's wrong to look to others for answers. If you pay a smart kid to do your maths homework, you're a cheat. If you find someone who's done the work before and use it, you're a cheat. If you have answers to problems and you sell them to others, you're a cheat.

Why on earth is all that called cheating? These are valuable skills as an entrepreneur. True entrepreneurs don't try to do their own homework, they find the best people they can afford to do it for them.

In school, if you see your friend has come up with a great answer to a problem, and you then copy it or improve upon it, you are labelled a copycat.

The kid who "improved upon a competitor's best practices" gets punished and nothing happens to the kid who left his "intellectual property unprotected."

We should punish the child who created valuable answers but carelessly left them to be discovered by the competition. That would more accurately reflect the real world today.

New Idea: Smart People Surround Themselves With Smarter People

Being smart in business is about finding the best people to work with you. You don't show how smart you are by having every answer; you show how smart you are by having access to every answer.

In business we reward the person who can find the answers quickly and who can use them to innovate in a new way. Why not at school? Why were you taught that this sort of behaviour is wrong?

The reason is simple. School is designed to create industrialized workers, not entrepreneurs.

If you went to school, you are probably riddled with old ideas that don't serve you in the new times we're entering. In the next chapter we will expose some more of them and attempt to flush a few out. If you are ready to get rid of some old industrial worker ideas and replace them with dynamic entrepreneurial ideas, then read on.

ACTIVITY: SELFISH LITTLE PLEBS

Let's play a game.

Pick a number. This number is an amount of money you want to spend in the next 12 months. It should be a number that at least satisfies all your wants and needs for the next year but isn't greedy.

Imagine that any number you write, as if by magic, will be yours to do with as you wish without further conditions. You can write any amount you want as long as you aren't greedy.

Choose the amount you want and write it down:

$ _____

NOTE: *Do it now, don't read on until you've got a number in mind.*

How much did you choose? Was it twice your salary, three times or did you go wild and write down something like a telephone number?

The instructions were clear. You had to choose a number that isn't "greedy."

If you wrote down a number less than a billion dollars I'm disappointed and we have a lot of work to do on your "empire building" mindset. Less than a billion indicates that you are too greedy and selfish to be fully functional in the Entrepreneur Revolution.

TOO "GREEDY" AND "SELFISH"!?

Why would I accuse you of that (if you wrote down less than a billion)? After all, if you are like most people your number was probably modest, you didn't ask for vast sums, you were reasonable.

Well, here is the thing. I said "an amount that would satisfy all your wants and needs."

If you only thought about your own personal desires, you're amount would be a small amount. It would be greedy. If you thought about your family, the amount would be bigger but still fairly small. If you thought about the big issues we face as a planet your amount would have been trillions!

Choosing a bigger amount would allow you to impact more people.

I am really hoping you have wants and needs that extend past you and your family. I hope you want to save rainforests, end hunger in faraway countries, influence government policy, set up foundations, empower people, rescue animals or something much bigger than yourself.

You just can't do that with an amount like £5 million.

With £5million you could have a nice home, a nice car, a nice holiday, make a nice little donation and invest a nice little amount for your future and pay some nice taxes.

That is it. You're barely able to do nice things for your extended family, your community, your local elderly, your local environment.

My answer is a little different.

I answer that question like this:

"I want the most amount of money that I can receive as a result of me being true to my authentic passions and inspirations."

If I am lucky enough to be like Bill Gates and my passion makes me a billionaire then I will rise to the challenges that billions calls for. I may also do what he did and run one of the biggest charitable foundations on the planet too ... if that is my authentic passion.

If my passion makes only a small amount of money but I am self-governing, free and I am an inspiration to myself and others then I will accept that too.

The important point is that it's not selfish to have a lot of spare time or a lot of spare cash. It's selfish to indulge all of your time doing something that neither serves or inspires anyone and then make a boring amount of money that only barely compensates you for your time.

THE POOR MINDSET IS THE GREEDY MINDSET

If you ask a rich person, "What would you do for £1000?" they would say, "It's not about the money."

If you ask a poor person, "What will you do for £1000?" they quickly demonstrate how easily they are bought. For a £1000 most people will give up the best part of their week for a vision that doesn't inspire them, working with people they barely care about and perform a role that is repetitive and dull. Most people will stay in a job they hate if the money is good enough.

In my opinion it is the poor minded person who is greedy for money, addicted to money; a slave to the filthy lucre.

It is the people with a rich mindset who are mostly indifferent to the stuff. They are only interested in their vision, their passion, their companions, their adventure.

In the Entrepreneur Revolution, you must be true to your convictions. If you're easily bought, you'll end up stuck in a dead-end job.

A STATE OF MONEY OR A STATE OF MIND?

Of course, it is all just a state of mind. However, it affects your most important decisions. It is a choice you can make at any time. Naturally, you will need a vision, a passion, an adventure ... but that will come later in this book. For now I still have a few points I need to make.

ACTIVITY: WHAT DO YOU DO FOR A LIVING?

What do you currently do for a living? Write it down:

_____

NOTE: *Don't read on until you have written down your answer.*

What did you write? Did you put down sales executive, area manager, apprentice plumber, tree surgeon, town planner, activist or architect?

Did you write down your job? Your occupation? Your source of income?

Why? Why did you write that? Why do most people think that what they do for income is what keeps them alive.

It's not! What keeps you alive is not your job title.

If you ask an American Inuit tribesman what he does for a living he will look at you strangely and say, "I breathe."

At least in the short term. After that I guess he will need some water, some good food, a good night's rest and an active day filled with a sense of adventure to keep him living.

After 200 years of conditioning we now answer with our job title.

The factory owners of the Industrial Revolution wanted their staff to be clear of one thing: "working in my factory keeps you alive, I give you your living." They wanted us to fear leaving the factory so they could pay people just enough to survive.

This is now a silly belief. Are you really scared of stopping breathing, or having access to water, food and shelter? I gave up my fear of that a long time ago. If you are reading this book you are probably lucky enough to be in the small percentage of the world's population that will not starve or go thirsty even if you really mess up. You have family, friends and welfare to fall back on until you get your wits about you.

In the Entrepreneur Revolution we kiss goodbye to this irrational survival fear of "not having enough to live." We have built up a fear that what we do for income is keeping us alive; but now we must move beyond it. It isn't logical and it doesn't serve us anymore.

It is an idea that the wealthy families don't have. If you asked Prince Charles what he did for a living he would probably be quite confused. When you explained that you were asking about how he sustained his place in the economy, he would tell you that he is royalty and has an empire and he reigns over it. It's unlikely he thinks he "works at the palace for a living."

Even self-made people are different. They all hate being asked that question. As an entrepreneur who's passionate about their business it doesn't feel like you're doing things to "make a living" and survive. The truth is you do a lot of stuff and it all seems to be in service of a vision you have. The truth is that wealthy people kind of "reign" over their little empires more than they "work for a crust."

If you asked me what I physically do for income my answer isn't so simple. I now have multiple business interests,

I am an international public speaker, I'm an author, I have investments … it is my little empire.

And, more to the point, it's not about the income! I do this stuff because it's in line with my vision, it's part of my adventure and I am inspired to do it. It just so happens that it produces income as well.

None of it makes me feel like I'm scraping out a living. I don't have to show up for work; I want to play this game.

So the big takeaway from this little chapter is simple.

We need to start thinking differently. We must stop thinking like workers and start thinking like entrepreneurs.

When you think about what you do for a living you start to think about your passion, your purpose and your vision. Don't think about your job, your income and your pension plan.

When you think bigger you will cease to be an unimportant worker who's surviving, you'll become an entrepreneur who is building an empire.

CHAPTER 4

MEET YOUR ENTREPRENEUR BRAIN

Your brain controls the way you think and the way you think controls what you do.

What you do, largely gives you the results you see in the outside world (including your bank balance, your house, your car, the types of holidays you go on and the difference you make).

So, if you want to consistently make things happen, it's vitally important that we take a look at the brain and how it's wired.

The brain is incredibly complex, and an exciting piece of kit to learn about properly. If you happen to be a brain-scientist forgive me for oversimplifying things but what I am about to discuss is designed to be useful for entrepreneurs rather than accurate to brain-scientists.

There are three key parts of your "entrepreneur brain":

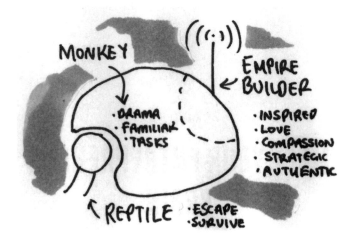

1. **The Reptile:** the survival part of your brain that has you see the world as a dangerous place where most people and most things can't be trusted. Its main purpose is to make sure that you can escape and survive any dangerous or stressful situation.

2. **The Monkey:** the functional worker part of your brain that has you see the world as a set of challenges and problems for you to play with and explore while you ride the emotional highs and lows that they *make* you feel.

3. **The Empire Builder** (or **Humanitarian** if you prefer): the empire builder/humanitarian part of your brain has you see the world as a deeply connected place that you can transform in a meaningful way.

DON'T LET THE REPTILE RUN YOUR LIFE

If you operate from the primitive, survival part of your brain, you can expect to live like a reptile. Reptiles don't have many friends, they eat flies, they don't evolve and they feel the cold when the winters of life come around.

Operating from the survival brain gives you more scarcity in the times we are living in. This part of the brain has no empathy for others, a skill that is vital in "value creation." The reptile isn't able to reason effectively and it has no concept of time. It's not a logical or strategic part of the brain, it's programmed to seek out situations that seem good for immediate survival with as little effort as possible.

Unfortunately it's easily fooled in these modern times. It's the part of the brain that will gamble on slot machines for hours on end, trading small coins for the hope of many coins, but it will never compute the folly of this activity.

It's the part of the brain that will hope for "passive income" and will sacrifice relationships and genuine opportunities in exchange for a shot at "having an endless stream of 'flies that land in your mouth' every day on their own."

The reptile believes the only resources that exist are those it can touch right now. If it can't see money, there's no money. If it can't see food, there's no food.

The reptile will destroy everything around itself if it thinks it will bring an immediate benefit to its survival. If you have ever lashed out at someone close to you, if you have ever smashed something valuable or sent a venomous email that later cost you dearly, it was you "going reptile."

The monkey brain

The monkey brain isn't much better than the reptile brain if you want to achieve success as an entrepreneur.

If you operate from the purely functional part of your brain, you will live like a monkey. You will have friends and you will be able to perform repetitive tasks, but most of what you do will not be very meaningful in the long term. You will enjoy nit-picking, and you will stay amused with very simple things.

The monkey brain loves to experience peak emotions like anger, sadness, happiness, surprise, sexual arousal and excitement. You can keep the monkey brain occupied for years by just stimulating peak emotions on a daily basis.

The monkey believes the only resources that it can access are those it's been told it can access. If you tell the monkey it earns £45,000 a year, it believes that's all there is. If you tell the monkey it has a credit card limit of £3500, that's it until a letter arrives from the bank saying that it's now £4000!

If you've ever gotten addicted to drama, caught up in meaningless repetitive endeavors or become a real party animal – that was you "going monkey."

THE EMPIRE BUILDER

If you want to build an empire, you need to access your empire building brain.

If you operate from the empire builder part of your brain you will live like an emperor. You will develop a space that is truly your own, people will be honored to share

conversations with you, you will solve big important problems and make a difference to many people.

The empire builder part of your brain has great amounts
of empathy, logic, reasoning and higher consciousness.
These are all great skills for building an empire.

You're empire builder brain has a capacity, quite literally,
to love the world. It can connect with people and events over
vast distances. It can calculate future events, it can draw
unique insights from your own past or even the stories of
others and naturally devise strategies. It's wise beyond the
comprehension of the monkey or the reptile.

While reptiles believe in resources they can touch and
monkeys believe what they are told, the empire builder
believes in the resources it can have influence over.

An empire builder believes that their empire grows
when they have greater influence over resources but they
care not who technically "owns" the resource.

Richard Branson sees the media as a resource because he has mastered such influence over the media, but he doesn't own it.

If you have ever had moments of pure inspiration where you feel anything is possible, you want to start a movement and do something meaningful for humanity, you were having an "empire builder" moment.

Here's the problem. The brain was built in such a way that the lower parts of the mind can shut down the higher parts. If the reptile brain is overstimulated it shorts-out the monkey and empire builder, and reptile takes over.

In a survival situation, you don't want to empathize with your attacker, nor do you want to make friends with it. You want to do what's needed to survive and nothing else. So the reptile is in charge when you feel your survival is immediately threatened.

If the reptile part of the brain returns to calm again, the mammal brain takes over and gets on with its feeble monkey existence that revolves around repetitive tasks and fluctuating emotions. The monkey brain is in charge when you do not feel like your survival is immediately threatened but when you're stimulated by peak emotions.

Provided the monkey brain stays stimulated, you cannot access the higher mind of the empire builder. The empire builder only comes out when you truly feel abundant, centred and complete in the moment.

This realization may start to give you insights into why society is set up the way that it is.

The people who ran the show in the Industrial Revolution did not want very many empire builders running around.

Many parts of society during the Industrial Revolution evolved to keep people from going into "survival mode" and tearing the streets up like savage reptiles. Governments set up provision for social security, pensions and healthcare because, without these things, the population might feel their very survival was under threat and end up burning down the city just trying to survive winter.

After survival is taken care of, the system is designed to keep people performing like well-trained little monkeys, who can perform mind-numbing, repetitive tasks for years on end. Good factory workers.

Most importantly, the system seems to have been set up to keep people from spending time in their higher mind – the empire building part.

Empire builders pose a threat to powerful industrialists; if an empire builder is in business they can take your market-share (like Richard Branson, Steve Jobs or Oprah Winfrey); or, if they are a humanitarian, they can liberate your workers (like Gandhi, Bobby Kennedy, Martin Luther King Jr).

In order to keep workers as workers, and to prevent them from rising up, two things must happen:

1. People must be convinced that they are able to survive. You must not threaten their survival in the immediate moment or they will turn savage and behave like reptiles; but you must ensure that people know that they aren't abundant *yet*.

2. People must be kept occupied with peak emotions while they aren't working so that they don't have a chance to access their higher mind. Not only will this prevent

people from becoming disruptive, but also the stimulated monkey brain loves to consume shiny new objects that it gets bored with rapidly. The stimulated monkey brain creates wonderful consumers in the economy.

Does this sound familiar? It should: it's exactly how the masses have been treated for the last 200 years. The mainstream news, entertainment and popular personalities all reinforce these two messages.

The traditional, mainstream media is an elegant way to keep most people in their monkey brain. It stimulates emotional highs and lows without immediately threatening your survival, which would throw you into your reptile brain.

If you look at the way we are bombarded by advertising and entertainment, it's no wonder so few people ever escape their monkey life of repetitive, meaningless tasks.

When you look at what's really going on in society, we have built global systems to keep people on the treadmill of being in the monkey brain!

If we examine almost every spiritual teaching that gives you a path to enlightenment, the advice is fairly simple – tune out from all the garbage for a while and give yourself a chance to access your higher consciousness!

Spiritual teachers often suggest going to a very safe place and fasting, meditating, being silent and celibate for a while. It's all about avoiding the stimulation of the monkey brain.

When people tune out from the noise, they give themselves a chance to access their inner empire builder. They tap into new ideas that could help people, and they discover vast resources they barely knew existed.

Accessing your inner empire builder isn't as hard as you might think. You need to do two things:

1. Convince yourself that you don't need anything – you are whole and complete in this moment and you're survival is not threatened in any way.
2. Avoid overstimulating yourself through emotional highs and lows (please note that I wouldn't class deep love or inspiration as a monkey brain emotion).

In the next chapter we will begin the process of awakening your empire builder and seeing just how much opportunity is surrounding you right now.

First, let's make sure you aren't feeding the reptile or stimulating the monkey too much. If you are, you'll spend all your time cleaning up the messes they make and there'll be none left for building your empire.

DO NOT STIMULATE YOUR REPTILE BRAIN!

If you want to destroy everything you have, stimulate your reptile mind regularly. But if you don't, then avoid engaging in negative self-talk whereby you tell yourself, over and again, how scarce things are and how tough life is. Stop telling yourself that you are barely surviving and there are no resources around you.

Don't keep an empty fridge or have no access to cash. Don't starve yourself of nutrition by eating cheap food. Don't deny yourself rewards for your efforts.

All of these things stimulate the reptile brain, which will push you to the brink of reptile behaviour. You will act aggressively to those who are closest to you, you will take stupid, short-term actions that come back to bite you and you will spiral out of control.

In order to try to stop the spiral you will construct an unattainable fantasy. In your fantasy, you might imagine yourself with passive income, retirement and big winnings.

In this fantasy, you probably don't have to do anything and money keeps rolling in. This fantasy is designed as a safety mechanism to try to stop you completely destroying yourself.

Unfortunately, the fantasy is a juvenile approach to life and it causes you to spend what little money or time you have on quick-fix solutions. You might join a multi-level-marketing operation that you won't then give any time to, you send money to a high-risk investment that you don't understand, you gamble or you blow money you don't have trying to create the fantasy.

It's easy to spot these reptile fantasies. They are typically presented to you as:

- **Passive income.** The reptile imagines that money comes from a source that requires no time, energy, effort or focus. The empire builder knows that making money and building a successful business will always require energy, time and effort. However, if you are dedicated to a meaningful cause it will be fulfilling, rewarding and ethical.

- **Retirement.** The reptile wants you to squirrel away money that you believe you will live on after you are too old "to hunt or gather." The empire builder never wants to retire, but looks to making a contribution for as many years as possible.
- **Multiple streams of income.** The reptile enjoys fantasizing about money coming from many sources, thus "safeguarding your food supply." The empire builder loves to focus on earning money from sources that fit perfectly with your mission and your vision; if it's one source or twenty, the empire builder cares not.
- **Big wins.** The reptile likes the idea of making all the money you need for the rest of your life in one hit. The empire builder doesn't try to get everything done in one hit, because it realizes that consistently creating regular wins creates the big jumps.
- **Entitlements.** Your reptile brain believes there's money that "should rightfully be yours." The empire builder believes that money is energy and will flow towards people who earn the right to utilize it best.
- **Providers.** The reptile wants a person or organization who will take care of you and then you won't need to worry about money. The empire builder is looking for organizations, causes and people to provide for.
- **Financial freedom.** The reptile imagines a time when you will not need to be responsible for money and thus be free from it. The empire builder recognizes and embraces the need to tackle the financial complexity that's created along with wealth.

Of course, all of these are juvenile concepts created by clever people who know how to sell ideas to reptiles and monkeys.

The only people who have these things are empire builders. However, they don't even relate to these concepts. They just think about building an empire.

For starters, empire builders never retire. They do all they can to work as long as they can – often they stop "working" just weeks before they die.

They don't see themselves as beneficiaries of passive income or multiple streams of income. They see they are in service of one growing empire that has much to be cared for.

They don't go for easy, quick wins. They take on the big challenges and, when they do have a big win, they find another big challenge to take on next.

They don't seek out financial freedom, they manage financial complexity. They don't look for a provider, they look for opportunities to provide for others.

Don't be a monkey

Living a monkey life is easy. Almost the whole of society wants you to do this. Often, it's your parents, your teachers, your government and your friends who want you to live by the monkey brain rules. They might say things to you like:

"Get a good job, settle down, fix your mortgage, don't rock the boat and put that dream off until you retire."

This is the monkey anthem. It's more than just an anthem – it's the day-to-day noise that is deafening when you realize how loud it's playing.

Even when you do try to tune out, a hundred things will show up and try to tune you back in.

The news, the media, the advertising industry, organized religion, workplaces and the government are all beating the same drum. It's designed to keep you marching to that drum.

It might feel nice to march to that drum at times. I've often envied those people who can do it. In times when my journey got tough, I wondered what it would be like to have a regular paycheck, a planned holiday break and to trust in the government and an employer to look after me in retirement. I imagine it must be bliss to those who haven't woken up their empire-builder brain. Like you have.

If you want to live like a monkey, ride the highs and lows of your emotions. When you get bored, create pointless drama. When the drama is all too much, throw in the towel and run off on the quest for the simple life.

If you want to live as a monkey, settle. Settle for a safe little house with a manageable little mortgage. Settle for a menial job that you could do in your sleep and pays a basic little survival wage. Settle for answers that don't make sense. Settle for self-serving institutions that take advantage of what little spare time and money you do have.

If that sound's unbearable, then keep reading. The alternative is to take your life up a gear and live as an empire builder.

To see Daniel talk about the entrepreneur brain visit:
www.entrevo.com/talk-brain

CHAPTER 5

HOW TO BE AN EMPIRE BUILDER – TEN CHALLENGES TO KICKSTART YOUR ENTREPRENEURIAL TALENTS

You now have a problem. If you are reading a book like this, you've probably already woken up the empire builder and it makes you restless.

You now yearn to do big, meaningful work. You want to cause an impact. You want progress and transformation.

This will not go away; it will get worse if you don't act upon it. This book is going to move you in the direction of a successful empire builder. If you trust my process, you won't just wake up your inner empire builder – you will live that way.

Rather than just talking about this mindset stuff (because I do appreciate that the mere fact you're reading this book is evidence you're already on the path), I want to give you some real-life challenges that will automatically start to break you out of the monkey brain system and begin to activate your empire builder.

Let's begin by doing something crazy.

I'm going to introduce you to ten tasks that are designed to challenge you. These tasks aren't theory. As you'll see, I've done each of them myself.

I've recommended these ten tasks to numerous friends and consistently the feedback is that they are nothing short of transformational.

As you read through these tasks it might be easy just to keep reading on without putting them into practice.

If you do keep reading, make sure you come back to these tasks as soon as possible and complete them.

These ten tasks aren't just fun things to read about, they are tasks to be completed. You will need to "do" these things to get the lessons.

Even if you think you can imagine what it would be like to complete these tasks – do them for real.

I promise you that, if you do, you will rapidly begin to flush out the industrialized worker mentality and open yourself up to a world of new opportunities. Magic will happen.

Knowing is not enough, we must apply.
Willing is not enough, we must do.
Bruce Lee

CHALLENGE 1: MAKE THREE CALLS

Begin something bold without knowing how, exactly, it will work out. You might want to plan an event, you might want to start producing a song, you might want to introduce yourself to that person you've been admiring and just say "Hi, how are you today?" Whatever it is, don't plan too far ahead, begin it and let it unfold AFTER you're in too deep. Make three phone calls and see what happens.

Let me take you back to the beginning of my entrepreneurial journey and walk you through some critical lessons I had along the way.

In the first year of university, my best mate Marcus and I came up with an idea to run a dance party for 15–17 year olds. The more we researched it and created clever and cheap ways to market the party, the more it seemed like an entirely valid idea.

I was excited but didn't know what to do next. I called up my dad, explained the situation and asked him what I should do; and he said "make three calls."

His suggestion was simple: make three phone calls to see if anyone else is interested in your idea. Not friends, not family, but three people who will either advance the idea forward or tell you why it's not for them.

My first call was to a warehouse shed company that had a big green building across the street from my local park. They told me that it wasn't a suitable venue and that they tried to have an 18th birthday party there once and it was a disaster. They suggested I call an actual nightclub venue.

My second call was more ambitious. I called the top nightclub in town.

"Hi Mr General Manager," I said in my most professional voice. "I am from a dance party promotions company and we have selected your venue as a possible venue for our next big gig for under-18s. You're normally closed on a Tuesday night so we were thinking about running something in the first week of school holidays with you."

To my amazement he didn't hang up on me, nor did he get excited. He simply asked me to fax through a proposal and then organize a time to meet with him through his assistant.

"Well I can't send you a proposal today because I am out of the office, but I will have one to you by lunch time tomorrow."

My third call was back to my dad to find out what a proposal was.

We met with the nightclub manager and he agreed to run the party. As we walked out the door, he asked if we had thought about radio ads.

We didn't have any money for radio ads but we used my dad's advice again and made three calls to local radio stations.

To our surprise we secured $4000 of free advertising in exchange for the naming rights of the party. The radio station suggested we should get some prizes from retail stores. We made three more calls and found retailers who were happy to give us over $1000 worth of prizes.

The retail stores suggested we have a fashion parade. We made three calls and found that one of the cutest girls in our class was a model who knew how to run a fashion parade. She suggested I also take her on a date some time and I made three calls to brag to my friends!

Our party was a huge success and my business partner and I both walked away with more cash than we could carry that night.

This became our sideline business and we were both able to make good spending money while at university.

On that first day, I never knew how it would unfold, I just made those calls to see what would happen next. I hadn't a clue what we would be getting ourselves into but it felt great to begin it. With each step forward the next steps appeared and before long we had an exciting result.

I'm not saying you should be reckless, I'm saying that it's impossible to know how things will pan out until after you begin. Take the first steps, pick up the phone and put yourself out there.

Your inner empire builder is OK with sitting in the tension of uncertainty. The empire builder knows that resources show up when they are needed and normally not beforehand.

Empire builders believe that they have access to any resources that exist on the planet, whenever they need it, and that they only need to have the right conversation to get them.

To begin this task, simply pick up the phone, send some emails and arrange some meetings. Begin the conversation without knowing where it will lead you.

The empire builder is OK stepping into the unknown and having an adventure. The empire builder sees the whole world as a stage and everyone as a fellow player in the game of life.

The empire builder isn't scared, but the monkey and the reptile get terrified if they think you're not able to survive, or if there's no money for the little luxuries later on in life. If they feel threatened, the reptile and the monkey will do everything they can to hold the empire builder back.

CHALLENGE 2: GET YOUR MONKEY A BANK ACCOUNT

Set up a new bank account and put at least 10% of all the money you earn into that account. This "monkey account" helps you to feel OK about taking risks, and will eventually stop you from needing to go do boring, familiar tasks. Don't touch that money; its purpose is nothing more than to become part of "your wealth." This wealth-building plan will be an essential key for keeping the monkey and the reptile off your back.

After the success of our first dance party, my best mate and I were thoroughly convinced that we were going to be successful entrepreneurs. We talked endlessly about how, one day, we would have expensive cars, big boats, and houses all over the world. We were planning out our dreams and we were excited.

Marcus's dad, Vac, took us aside and gave us some interesting advice. He said "be sure to put 10% aside and then you can go blow the rest on whatever you want."

It was shocking advice coming from an adult. Weren't we meant to invest it all, or pay off some debt (not that we had any), or save it up for a distant rainy day?

Vac was a clever businessman, and this was his best advice: to enjoy our earnings whilst putting aside 10% of everything into a separate, wealth-building account. He said, "if you just keep 10% of everything you earn, you'll build wealth. Having wealth puts you in a position to make better choices with your life."

The monkey brain is risk adverse. It just wants to do repetitive things with a little bit of drama mixed in.

The people around you will tell you how risky it is to go and do big things like start a business. Having a safe stash of money, that just keeps growing, helps you to reason with your monkey brain.

You need your monkey brain to feel safe that this money will not be used by the empire builder for any "hairbrained dreams or schemes." The money you put aside can never be used for business, spending or risky investments. It's for boring stuff like cash, property, shares and metals.

The monkey and the reptile need to know your future is being taken care of, so this account will please the part of you that's conservative and safe and concerned about your long-term survival.

I set up a special account with my bank called "the monkey account" and 10% of my earnings went into it.

To this day these earnings sit around in boring investments – nothing too sexy, nothing too risky.

However it just keeps ticking along. I bought one set of shares for $12 and they were at $45 the last time I checked. I put some money into a fund that always seems to go up by 5% a year. I've bought some precious metals and they seem to be going up in value too.

I hardly look at it and it always shocks me to see how much it adds up to over time. It makes me feel very calm to know that I have money to fall back on if I need it.

The other thing to note is that when you put a bit of money aside you don't miss it. I have lived on yachts, had penthouse apartments, travelled the world, eaten in the best restaurants and driven prestige cars. In time, you'll see that your empire builder plan is going just fine without your little monkey money.

CHALLENGE 3: STOP SPENDING TIME WITH PEOPLE WHO BRING YOU DOWN

Start making friends with more people who inspire you. Spend more time having conversations with people who bring out the best in you. Make a list of people you currently spend a lot of time with and decide who can stay and who might need to go.

You become just like the people you have conversations with. These people determine the dominant ideas you ponder, the opportunities you notice and the resources you can access.

If you do not have any people on your list who inspire you, you're better off spending time out networking in inspirational places trying to find some.

Today I'm fortunate to spend a lot of my time with very inspiring people. I talk regularly with people who run exciting, fast-growth enterprises, people who lead charities and people who've achieved remarkable things and continue to address meaningful challenges.

Most of my insights come from an ongoing conversation with a peer group of empire builders.

One of the reasons I dropped out of university was because I realized that most people I spent time with were playing small. At the end of my first year in university I became aware that most people I met were struggling to survive. I remember talking to a business lecturer who shared the fact that he and his wife were really struggling to pay rent. This scared me. Why am I learning from a guy who's struggling to pay rent?

I could see this was only going to make me believe that playing small was normal.

So I decided to set out and find some mentors to shadow. I figured that if I could spend time with wealthy, dynamic, inspiring people, I might actually figure out what they do differently.

It was a frightening move to leave my friends and peers. I was afraid that I would be alone and wouldn't fit in with another crowd. My parents were both the first in their families to have a university degree and now I was going to become a "dropout."

When I was 19 years old I went to work for a friend of a friend named Jon, a very successful businessman and marketeer.

Jon's company promoted and ran events all over Australia. He had a big house, a vibrant family and he was engaged in meaningful work. He wore board shorts and sandals most of the time, woke up when his kids did, played lots of games and was great fun to be around.

When he asked me to join his team of "inspired sales legends," I laughed, because it was a very different way of explaining a job compared to the door-to-door roof insulation company sales team I had been working in on weekends. They simply called me a "door-knocker."

The other people who worked for Jon were all interested in achieving big, exciting and meaningful things too. The inspired conversations began and my mind tuned into all sorts of new opportunities.

I went from having regular conversations about grocery bills, rent and university deadlines to goals, dreams, plans and revenue targets.

After a few weeks I knew that I wanted to learn more so I asked Jon if he could teach me about marketing and business. He agreed and the lessons began.

He taught me about sales, marketing, conducting meetings, doing deals and building wealth. He also taught me how to treat money differently.

CHALLENGE 4: CARRY CASH

Carry £1000 on you at all times. If £1000 isn't enough to make
you a little bit uncomfortable, carry the amount you'd love to
earn in a day.

One day, my new mentor Jon asked me how much money I
considered to be a lot. After some thought I replied "There's
not much a guy can't do on $1000 a week."

He laughed, and said that if I was only making $10,000
worth of sales a week (I was on 10%) then he wouldn't keep
me on in his company. This excited me no end.

He then asked me to do something quite strange, which
had a powerful impact on my life.

Jon asked me to get my hands on $2000 and bring it back
to him. I told him that I had $100 in cash, $500 in the bank
and I had $1000 limit on my credit card. He said, "go ask your
dad for the rest or something, just bring me $2000 tomorrow."

I somehow got my hands on this vast sum of money and
brought it back to him. Without much of a care he took it off
me, stuck a bulldog clip on it and said "carry that in your
pocket at all times."

It was wild. I was walking down the street feeling that, at
any moment, a gang of ninjas would jump me and steal my
entire net worth. I was nervous and excited all at once ... and
my hand never left my pocket for the first few weeks (better
safe than sorry).

Then, one day, something strange happened. I was walking past a jewelry store and I saw an Omega watch. It was
awesome!

"It's $2000 ... you can't afford that" said my monkey brain. "Wait a second ... I have $2000 in my pocket ... I can afford it if I want," my empire brain replied.

After a brief conversation with myself, I realized that, even though I could afford it, I would choose to wait until I had earned it. I decided that when I had turned over $1 million in my own business I would buy it as a reward. That felt right, and it also made me feel empowered that I had made this decision on my own rather than feeling powerless in view of the watch's price tag.

Over the following 12 months this became a regular occurrence. I would notice something I thought I could not afford and then realized that I actually had enough money in my pocket to buy most things.

All of a sudden, I was in the driver's seat. I had the power over the things and not the other way around. I had lost my emotional charge on them, I had also lost my charge on the idea that $2000 was a lot of money; it's just how much I carried in my pocket!

It's almost impossible to "go reptile" when you have a wad of cash in your possession. The reptile simply won't wake up unless it's worried about immediate survival issues, or unless it spots a big, potential windfall.

With cash in your pocket, you won't be worried about your immediate survival and you won't be as susceptible to juvenile promises of easy windfalls.

In the first year working for Jon I went from earning $800 a month, as a broke university student, to earning $12,000 a month doing something that I considered fun; plus I was living in a gorgeous beach location. Few people take this sort of a jump so quickly, and I believe that the $2000 in the pocket was a big part of that shift.

Carry cash so you don't ever feel your survival is at stake. It will also allow you to confront your issues around money and recalibrate how much your brain thinks is a lot. This activity will do more for you than reading all the money books or attending all the money seminars.

CHALLENGE 5: BUY TWO LUNCHES PER WEEK FOR PEOPLE YOU DON'T YET KNOW

Take two new people out to lunch each week and pick up the bill.

I was told that I needed to build a good network of people around me who weren't customers, clients or old friends. To help with this, I had to select two new people a week to take out for lunch … at my expense. This was tough in the beginning, but wonderful later on.

Initially, I couldn't think of anyone who would want to go to lunch with me, who I would be willing to pay for. I was stalemated by my lack of confidence and my lack of money.

But I had to come up with two per week, so I just started asking people who I would never have thought would join me for lunch. Business owners, investors, accountants and even the occasional attractive girl if I was feeling particularly cheeky.

You'll be surprised at how many great people respond favourably when you say "Can I take you out for lunch next week, it's on me, I don't know you well enough but I'm sure there's plenty of good reason we should be talking."

To my amazement, people I invited were always quite happy to go out to lunch. I listened to their stories, got great advice, fresh ideas and found myself learning all sorts of new things. I learned to connect with people and discovered what people are going through in life beneath the surface.

I was developing a network and I was able to start introducing people, which made me feel even more valuable.

When I got on the phone to make a sales call I had all sorts of stories to share and I was speaking from experience and a genuinely inspired place. People would listen to me ... and I made a lot of sales!

Often I would get introduced to people as well. I would get referrals, opportunities and advice. Taking people out to lunch wasn't an expense, it was making me money.

When you begin to do this, you will find out very quickly that taking people out to lunch isn't going to be an expense. Having a network builds your net worth more than almost anything else.

CHALLENGE 6: TUNE OUT FROM THE NEWS

Give up on all traditional media and news for a while. No papers, no radio, no TV. Feel free to Google stories or to look through Twitter and Facebook, but for at least 90 days avoid traditional media.

On the weekends I would walk down to the local cafe on the beach and order breakfast and a juice and read the newspaper, to catch up on the rest of the world that I had missed out on while I was busily building my little empire through the week.

It was terrible: war, death, accidents, failing businesses, crashing stock markets, rising interest rates, rapists and murderers. This stuff was everywhere!

Well, it wasn't everywhere; a lot of it was happening in other parts of the world. Very few disasters were happening in my little beachside township, hardly any murderers had killed people I knew personally and virtually none of the wars were taking place in my local area.

When I took stock of this fact I realized that almost none of the news was relevant to my life at all. These events were going to happen with or without my involvement. Even though I was aware of these news stories I wasn't going to reactively do much about it, other than to ride the emotional highs and lows of the story.

I had been led to believe that I needed to be up to date with these world events in order to function in society. I'd been told that news was important and it helped to shape my mind as a free thinker. I discovered that this isn't as true as it once was and that carefully selected books and websites are better.

With encouragement from a mentor, I decided it was safe to tune out from the news. I bought good books for the weekend at the cafe and to completely be carefree from the world events of politics, wars, death and destruction.

And guess what happened? Nothing!

I didn't get surprised by the phantom boogeyman that the papers had been warning me about. I didn't lose all my money in a stock market crash that had been repeatedly mentioned on TV. No national draft picked me to fight a war that I hadn't been up to date on ... absolutely nothing happened ... except I felt good!

I felt light and empowered all the time. Occasionally, someone would say "aren't you worried about flying?" and I would say "No, why would I be?" and they would look at me as if I was either a heroic champion for getting on with things under pressure, or a loony who simply didn't understand the imminent threats associated with the new insurgence of terrorists.

Either way, I made it through the dangerous world just fine.

My monkey brain was terrified of tuning out from the news. It needed the emotional highs and lows and, in the first few weeks, it really kept nagging at me to get a newspaper or switch on the television for an update.

After a while, my monkey brain calmed down and I felt OK about living in a world without a daily download of the statistically improbable disturbances to the planet.

When you tune out from the news, you will probably feel anxious that you're missing out on something. Quickly you will discover that, if anything does relate to you, someone will tell you about it. After a while, you will be shocked at how much energy you once gave to this thinly veiled form of entertainment.

Instead of getting worried about world events, I stayed inspired and kept on doing things that worked.

I came to discover that my own life was more important than the stories presented to me by some newsroom editor.

When I focused on my own life I did things that were newsworthy myself. My life was becoming more interesting and I put value on my own unfolding story.

So much was happening that I decided to start writing it down.

CHALLENGE 7: KEEP A JOURNAL

Start a journal. Make lists of high-value tasks, write down your goals, draw pictures, write sales copy and project your future. Keep track of your thoughts and mark down your milestones. Every empire builder needs to endlessly explore ideas, plans, goals, targets and keep track of important stories.

Every mentor I've ever had keeps a journal on them. It shows up at every meeting, it goes on holiday with them, it rides shotgun next to them in the car and sleeps by their bed at night.

There are so many ideas buzzing about in the empire builder brain. Brilliant, multi-million dollar ideas seem to come thick and fast showing up virtually every day – almost like a replacement for the newspaper.

These ideas need to be explored on paper. Calculations need to be done, resources need to be explored, lists of missing pieces need to be accounted for and diagrams need to be sketched.

No matter how smart you are, you need a journal.

My first mentor, Jon, insisted that I keep a journal. He would give me a magazine and tell me to rewrite the ads in a way that was more customer focused.

He would get me to work out projected revenues on campaigns we were running. He would ask me to list all the goals I wanted to achieve by my 21st birthday, and to make a tally of all the things I was most grateful for to date.

My journals filled up quickly and, by writing these things down, I noticed that my mind was free to have even more ideas.

To this day I'm constantly surprised when I go back through my journals from years earlier. Quite regularly the things I had named as "big goals" were things I could tick off the list just 24 months later.

Get into the habit of writing in your journal. Even if you just sit with it open and make lists of things that come to your mind. If you've not kept a regular journal it can seem foreign to sit and write but, eventually, you wake up a very creative part of your brain that loves to express itself.

Here are some key things to write down to get you started:

- What are you most grateful for in your life so far?
- Who's been helping you recently whom you haven't acknowledged?
- What do you want to achieve before the end of the year?
- Which ten business ideas would you start if you had £100k to invest?
- Who can you take out to lunch this month?
- What have you noticed since carrying £1000 in your pocket?

Challenge 8: Plan Your Holidays First

Take out a yearly planner (I like giant Sasco wall planners) and put in the holidays you want to take. Blank out the time you'll be taking off in the coming year. Rule out the long weekends you plan on taking and the mid-week lazy days you want off.

This task is an exciting one and it will do wonders for you as an entrepreneur.

Most people plan their holidays around their work. They hope there will be some spare time and money for holidays each year. But you are not a robot, you're a human being with limited time to explore the earth.

The successful people I know plan their work around their holidays and so should you.

Start the year by blocking out at least 8–12 weeks of holiday time. Take out a big year planner at the beginning of the year and block out your holidays first. Work out where you want to go, how much you need to set aside and then reverse engineer your work to serve the lifestyle you want to live.

Why is this important? Firstly, it allows your brain to relax about "getting some downtime" because it knows the holidays are coming. This allows you to get so much done when you are working. It also allows your family and friends to relax about when they will be able to spend some real quality time with you. If your family know that there's a good ten weeks of planned holidays, they won't worry so much if you have to be home late or work through a weekend here and there.

Next, holidays also give you time to think. I have my best ideas on holiday. With some distance between me and the functional elements of my business, I get to play with the big picture and the really important stuff. It's amazing how powerful it is to get some time in nature, away from all the screens. Holidays recharge you.

Finally, your holidays ensure you have deadlines. It's amazing how much gets done the week before you take two weeks to go sailing with limited WiFi. The week before, you somehow move mountains so you can switch off and enjoy the trip.

For most of the last ten years, I've started the year by blocking out my holidays. There have been a few years where I forgot to do it proactively, and I ended up not taking my holidays.

As a result of this principle, I feel I've had an interesting multi-dimensional decade. As well as building businesses, I've had some great adventures. I've sailed Thailand, Vanuatu, the Mediterranean and the Australian coast. I've snowboarded the Alps, the Rockies, and in Japan and Australia. I've explored Asia and Indonesia. I've volunteered and raised funds in India and Africa. I've partied in Ibiza, Las Vegas, Bali and Morocco.

The years I took holidays were always much better than the ones I just worked. Better financially, better for my morale, better for connecting with people, better for big dreams and better for my health.

Don't skip this step. Find a way to make it happen.

CHALLENGE 9: GET STRUCTURED

Make an appointment with an accountant and a lawyer to discuss your business and wealth-building plans. Ask them to steer you in the right direction for tax planning, wealth protection and attracting investment.

Consider this:

- Empire builders use company structures and trusts to manage their wealth.

- Empire builders learn how the system works so they can legally structure themselves and live exactly how they want.

- Empire builders believe they should pay the minimum amount of tax legally required of them and not more.

- Empire builders believe it would be folly to expose their empire to the risk of being unfairly sued by an opportunistic low life.

- Empire builders believe they should build wealth in a way that encourages other empire builders to get involved. They create structures that are attractive to investors and high-performing people.

All of this takes planning.

From a young age I was encouraged to meet with accountants and lawyers to discuss these issues.

No one is born with an inbuilt knowledge of how legal and accounting systems operate. It's something you need to learn.

You spend 100% of your life interacting with these systems. It's crazy not to understand them.

Most people think they will set up a structure *after* they make a lot of money. Sadly, this doesn't work.

You must create a wealth structure before you make money. It's a nasty catch-22. Companies, trusts, accountants and lawyers all cost money and you have to spend this money before you have it.

Wealth structures are an investment and you need to find ways to build them.

I recommend that you talk to lawyers and accountants before you make a lot of money. Many lawyers and accountants will meet you for an hour, free of charge.

To complete this challenge you should set up several meetings with these business advisors to discuss your plans. Even if you don't go ahead with any of their suggestions, you will be more knowledgeable about your options.

CHALLENGE 10: GET YOUR ENTREPRENEURIAL TEAM IN PLACE

Build a team of people around you who can help you to implement your ideas and achieve the big goals you have for your future. No matter if you are starting out or you're already a millionaire, it will be the team you build today that will determine the results you get tomorrow.

There's no such thing as a self-made millionaire. In every case, people who are described as self-made are surrounded by a brilliant team of people.

Talking about your next big move in business is nice and it's important. However, the rubber won't hit the road for you until you're able to recruit key players onto your team.

I started out as a valuable player on my mentor's team, then I had to go out and build a team of my own.

It wasn't until I built a team that I was able to start my business.

If you are starting out, here's my draft pick for who you should have on day one:

1. A visionary – big picture focused, good at delegating, hardworking and can communicate the vision of the business and bring in new partnerships (probably you).

2. A graphic designer – can take the vision and create brochures, websites, sales forms, business cards, and make a business idea look tangible.

3. A sales person – someone who's genuine, likable and can ask that tough question "how would you like to pay for that?"

4. A Swiss army knife – someone who isn't 100% brilliant in any one thing, but can get most things done well enough. They are organized, flexible, frugal and detail orientated. They can do data entry if required, customer service calls, order supplies, book flights, fix most IT problems or quickly find someone who can.

5. A mentor – outside the business, successful, wise, been around the block and had few bloody noses, available for late-night chats over a glass of wine. This could also take the form of a mastermind group rather than just one person.

These people could be a mix of full-time staff that you hire, virtual staff paid by the hour or even people who are helping you out as a favour.

If you're already in business, with an existing team, this principle still applies. If you want to grow, you will need some new high performers. You'll know better than I do who you need next on your team but, rest assured, you got this far because of who you put around you, and you'll get where you're going for the same reason.

I have seen businesses start out with complex financial modeling, forecasts, projections and schedules, and big ticks in all the boxes from government agencies who supposedly know something about starting up. Despite all the planning, they fail hard and fail fast if they don't have a team to implement the plan.

Some of the best entrepreneurs I know are quite bad at putting business plans together, and tend to write notes on scraps of paper more often than they write detailed plans.

One thing they are good at, however, is recruiting the right people around them and building a culture where high performers want to stay.

Entrepreneurial teams might not always have a plan but they possess an amazing ability to pull things together under all sorts of conditions. They get sales in the door, deliver upon the promises of the business, keep costs down, start early, finish late, communicate powerfully and stand strong under pressure.

Make a list of people to have on your entrepreneurial team. Start keeping an eye out for a great sales person, a detail-oriented administrator, a customer service person, and so on.

You simply can't build a successful business on your own. You need to become a master at spotting the potential in everyone you meet.

To see Daniel talk about the ten challenges visit
www.entrevo.com/ten-challenges

DON'T SKIP THE TOUGH CHALLENGES

The tasks that I set out each have hidden lessons built in.

If any of these tasks really challenge you and you feel uncomfortable, try to dig deep and look for the underlying beliefs that make it so challenging. Over the years, I have seen these ten challenges bring up some strange beliefs in my clients.

What might you believe about money that prevents you from carrying it?

If you worry that you will lose it, explore why you feel you are irresponsible with money. If you are scared of being mugged, take a look at your belief that having money means attracting bad people and events.

What do you believe about yourself that stops you from associating only with inspirational people?

If you are worried that they won't like you, what makes you feel so unworthy? If you are afraid they will take advantage of you, explore why you believe successful people are manipulative.

What is it that makes you feel so uneasy about switching off from news, taking leaps into the unknown or planning great holidays?

Anything at all that comes up in your mind and stops you from implementing these ideas is worth taking a good look at.

Is it possible these limiting beliefs are holding you back in other areas of your life too? If so, you need to push through and do the toughest tasks first.

I promise you that these ten challenges will change your life, if only you are willing to step into the unknown and trust the process.

It's not easy going from the world of "industrialized factory worker" to the world of "entrepreneurial adventurer."

As we discussed, society has so many unspoken rules about what you should and shouldn't be doing. These ten challenges will most definitely feel uncomfortable at first because they deliberately rub up against these old rules.

In the Steven King movie *The Shawshank Redemption*, the main character spends close to two decades tunneling out of his prison to freedom. Inch by inch, he frees himself from the physical and psychological constraints of his maximum-security confines.

It's an inspiring movie for many people and it's a powerful metaphor. I've given you ten ways to tunnel out of the Industrial Revolution and into the freedom of the Entrepreneur Revolution. Take your time, keep digging and inch by inch you will be closer to a whole new level of freedom.

Get a coach, a mentor or join a group to hold you accountable if you need to, but push yourself to get the breakthrough you deserve. The juice will be worth the squeeze.

As you tunnel your way out of the industrialized system, sometimes you will catch a glimpse of what it's like living outside of the system and sometimes it will get tough.

No matter what, you must continue to lean in.

CHAPTER 6

LEAN IN

On a snowboard, it's common to feel tired, unstable, stuck, or out of your depth. Most newbie riders naturally lean back to try to escape the situation that's troubling them.

They secretly wish they were off the mountain. However, the minute you lean back, your feet wobble, you can't steer yourself and you find yourself face down in the snow. Leaning back causes you to lose balance completely. It hurts, it's humiliating, and it makes you want to get the hell off the mountain even more.

Experienced riders know that leaning back doesn't work. They know that if they want to have a good time they must overcome the urge to lean back. They must lean *in* to the mountain.

As soon as they lean in, they get stability, control and they get into the flow of things.

Most people are leaning back from their business, industry, job or even their life.

Secretly they are wanting things to be easier. They want to have the idea and get paid for being a visionary. This isn't how it works.

Empire builders are the ones who implement with excellence, not the ones who just sit around with nothing more than their lofty ideas.

Leaning back in your business or your life will cost you dearly.

Leaning back is when you start looking for an exit; it's when you want an old product just to keep on selling; it's when you get annoyed that you have competition. Leaning back is the lazy way, or the way of a coward.

True entrepreneurs lean in. When they have the chance to invest money in a smart way, they take it. If a great person becomes available they hire them. If a competitor shows up, they get fired up for the challenge of outperforming them.

When you lean in, you don't dream of retirement. You don't hope for an exit to show up. You hope to be better, you want your vision to show up and you dream of *never* retiring.

Leaning in means working with the best people, it means showing up with your game face on and leaving your doubts at the door.

Leaning in means taking the calculated risk, it means committing to being excellent, and to doing what it takes to solve whatever problems come along. It means spending time, money and energy when the opportunity comes along and then taking accountability for the results.

Leaning in is about pursuing your vision, loving your team, caring about the details and getting it right.

Leaning in is about wishing to be better, not wishing for things to be easier.

Strangely, leaning in produces an easier life.

Just like on a snowboard, when you lean in life gets easier. When you lean in, your business works, you attract a great team, your products sell. When you lean out, life is hard. When you lean in life shows up as easy, you have stability and you attract opportunity.

Leaning back from your world produces a difficult life. You end up falling for every gimmick because you are searching for an easy answer. Leaning back makes everyone else lean back: the people on your team are also looking for an exit, they are also wanting quick fixes and they are only giving 50% of their best game.

If you want the results, you'd better be leaning in.

CHAPTER 7

THE VERY ESSENCE OF SUCCESS

What makes some people successful while others struggle?

Why is it that some people in an industry are millionaires and other people in the same industry are just getting by?

Why is it that Kate Moss is paid millions to be a model, while other models, who are just as pretty, get paid $300 a day?

Why is David Blaine a millionaire street magician when other magicians just make enough for their next meal, despite knowing all the same magic tricks?

Why is it that Jonathan Ive gets millions to design products at Apple and other designers make $60 an hour?

I have three answers to this riddle but, before I tell you the first reason, make a list of all the traits you think the successful people have that the others don't.

Make a list of all the things that you think separate the highly valued and highly paid people from those just getting by. What do you think are the mystery ingredients that got them where they are today?

_____	_____
_____	_____
_____	_____

NOTE: *Don't read on until you have listed your answers.*

I hope you thought of a few things before reading on. In fact, if you haven't, please do so. You'll get more out of this book if you do.

If you are like most people you will put down words like: self-belief, determination, passion, character, leadership and decisiveness.

Great words but they all have a bit of a problem. They are not mutually exclusive.

I can take all those sorts of words and put them down onto a list and check them against the richest people on the planet and we would find that, sure enough, these words are quite relevant to them. These super success stories have courage, determination, passion, and all those things we mentioned.

The problem is, when I take those same traits and apply them to people who aren't so successful, I can find those qualities too. I can see determination in the eyes of the guy who works 70 hours a week; I can see belief in the network marketer who thrusts her sample pack into the hands of another unwilling contact; I can find plenty of passion in the engineer who arrives at work for another new challenge to tinker with.

It is the same list of traits, but some people are making it while others aren't.

So what is the real key to success? What is the one thing that sets all the big-time people apart from the small-time strugglers? What is the thing that, if the little guys had it, they would make it? The thing that all the big guys acknowledge and the little guys fail to think about?

There are three keys that all successful entrepreneurs need if they are going to make the most of their ideas, talents, opportunities and the times we're in.

Every entrepreneur will need:

1. Luck
2. Reputation
3. Vitality

In the sections ahead, I will explain the importance of each.

THE FIRST KEY: LUCK

LUCK!

"Luck ... you mean I read all this stuff to arrive at the first big key to success and it's LUCK!"

Sorry guys and gals, but luck is going to play a part in your life whether you like it or not. Hard work is not going to be your unique selling proposition, you simply couldn't work hard enough.

Your big break isn't going to come through more belief in yourself – just watch *American Idol* and you will see plenty of people with belief, passion, and courage ... who get turned down. Yep, the bad news is that *all* successful people have been wildly lucky!

The good news is that you are already born lucky. If you are reading this book, you had an education, you have money to buy books, you have time to read.

The other piece of good news is that you can cultivate luck. There are lucky places and unlucky places. There are lucky people to associate with and unlucky people you should avoid.

You also might not even see just how much luck is already showing up for you and has been showing up for you since the moment you were born.

The first key to luck is that you learn to recognize luck. If you can't even see how lucky you are already you will be blind to any good fortune that shows up in the future.

Here's how I discovered my luck.

I had just finished giving a talk over breakfast to about 100 wealthy Indian business owners at one of the most luxurious hotels in Mumbai, India.

Afterwards, the organizer asked me if I wanted to meet her friend, who ran a school in the slum area of Mumbai, and I enthusiastically accepted the offer not really knowing what I was in store for.

We caught a cab into the heart of the slum area. This wasn't just a few people doing it tough, this was millions of people living on top of each other; each person desperately seeking a better life, each struggling for survival without what I would consider the basics of clean water, electricity and a solid roof to sleep under.

I ventured into the school and met with a class of 40 vibrant students. The tin shed classroom was a sweltering sauna. Yet the kids were so eager to learn. They scribed out their alphabets with broken chalk on their slate. They listened enthusiastically to their teacher and they graciously accepted me being in their class.

Their clothes were little more than rags, probably thrown out by someone in the West for having a small rip or stain; now they were the only set of clothes these kids had.

As my day of touring ended, I got back into a taxi and headed to my next hotel. My cab crawled along in peak traffic and, with no air conditioning, the sweat rolled down my face. I sat for two hours, staring at scene after scene of poverty.

At one point, the cab passed an aid agency dumping barrels of clean water on the road, and dozens of people swarmed in to fill their drinking containers. One little boy, who must have been barely five years old, pushed a rusty tin can under the stream and gladly drank from it. It broke my heart to watch.

Then, after what seemed like hours in the cab, we rounded a corner to my five-star hotel, where the guards waved us through the gates.

On the other side were beautiful water features. In-numerable gallons of clean, drinkable water flowed from fountains and statues, sprinklers kept the pristine gardens green and a waterfall churned down an artificial rock face into the pools.

Although it was nothing I hadn't seen before, on this day I felt my heart tearing up just looking at it.

Emotional and overheated, I checked into the hotel. The receptionist recognized I was a speaker at the conference and offered me an upgrade. I was ushered to a "superior room" that was about four times the size of the school I'd just been in.

This was all becoming too much. I figured I'd better shower and cool off. As I turned the shower on, four water jets came to life and so did my eyes.

Tears streamed down my face. I had felt so closely connected to the children in the school, so welcomed and so happy to be with them. Now I was set in a scene that would be beyond their wildest dreams.

What's worse is that this wasn't a new scene for me. It was just another five-star hotel, cut and pasted like any other I'd stayed in on my travels.

In that moment, I discovered my luck. For the first time ever my eyes were open to how, every moment of my life, I had been living one of the luckiest lives in the history of humanity.

It suddenly hit me: I have water, education, food, housing and a free mind.

I have film makers spending millions to create entertainment for me on the off chance I might watch it. I have airlines running fleets of planes around the world on the off chance I want to fly. I have farmers preparing their best produce and sending it minutes from my front door.

I live in such a lucky time in history! Never before could people get their questions answered in seconds. Never in history could people communicate their ideas with so many others. Never has there been more finance, more resources, more exciting conversations.

Whichever way I look at it, I'm living a life more extravagant than the royal families throughout the ages. King Louis XIV would sit talking to me with his jaw open in amazement of what I have access to in my day-to-day life.

When all that really hit me I truly got it … "I'm so lucky!"

And so are you.

If you can't start with that, you will miss the luck that shows up next. The ability to acknowledge how lucky you already are, and to be grateful for it, allows you to see opportunities more clearly.

YOU CAN MAKE YOURSELF LUCKIER

Once you recognize how lucky you already are, the next step is to learn how to influence luck. You can coax it into your life and encourage it to show up.

You influence your luck when you show up in places that are luckier, when you spend time with people who are luckier, when you learn ideas that produce luck, when you get crystal clear on your vision and when you begin having lucky conversations.

Given the choice between doing another repetitive day at the office or going to an event that's full of inspired leaders, I will choose the event. It's luckier.

I don't know who I will meet or what will come of it but I do know that there's a good chance that something great will happen.

Given the choice of talking to someone who's convinced there are no opportunities out there, or talking to someone who's enthusing about an exciting future, I will talk to the person with an inspired outlook. It's luckier.

I don't know what exactly I will learn from them, I just know that I will probably discover something worth knowing about.

Given the choice between watching random TV or watching a riveting talk on TED.com I will watch TED. It's luckier.

Every day we are making choices that will either make us even luckier, or choices that repel the luck that is desperately trying to show up in our lives.

People want to be able to create success the same way a chef makes a pie. They want a recipe and a formula. They want to know what exactly to do in a step-by-step method.

Unfortunately, a huge part of the formula is that you have to be lucky. I hope I've convinced you that being lucky is actually something you are in control of. I hope I've also shown you that luck is already trying to beat down your door.

THE SECOND KEY: REPUTATION

We are moving into a time when everyone and everything is connected. In the Entrepreneur Revolution your most prized asset is your personal brand and reputation.

When somebody Googles your name, the first page of results is a clear indication of how the world sees you.

Is it clear what you do? Is it clear what you are good at? Can people see a photo or a video of you? Can they find testimonials? This is important stuff.

In a world where the most cutting-edge technology has been designed to leverage your message, you must build a profile and guard your reputation.

We live in a world where your reputation will follow you around for life. One seriously stupid decision will be searchable for a very long time if the story hits the internet.

Losing his reputation cost Tiger Woods over $25m in lost contracts in the short term. The long-term effects of his lost reputation could be over $100m. It's an extreme example. However, it illustrates a point that's relevant at all levels of business.

On the flip side, a great reputation will pick you up when you're down or even rescue your business. Richard Branson's reputation is so strong, his involvement in the failing bank Northern Rock helped to turn it around.

He says: "Your reputation is all you have in life – your personal reputation and the reputation of your brand. And if you do anything that damages that reputation, you can destroy your company."

In my first book, *Become a Key Person of Influence*, I discussed how I witnessed certain people become go-to people in their industry. These people then earned more money, had more fun and attracted more opportunity.

My first book became a best-seller. As a result, I was featured in the media and was offered considerable amounts of money just to turn up and speak at events around the world. Often, I would get paid more money for a 45-minute talk than most people earn in a month.

I've been offered shares in other peoples businesses because of my reputation and my profile.

As a result of my reputation and profile, I was approached by a major publisher to write the book you have in your hands.

So, a reputation and a profile are valuable assets that pay regular dividends. People who have a reputation receive inbound opportunities. Their phone rings every day with perfect projects. They don't have to chase constantly for their next paycheck, the money comes and finds them.

By far your most prized asset must be your reputation. It's an asset that will pay you well for life. Guard it, nurture it, make decisions with your reputation in mind because great entrepreneurs believe that money comes and goes but your reputation is permanent.

Consider all the people you know who make great money, who live exciting lives, who have influence and success in abundance. Unless they inherited it, I can guarantee you that they are well known in their field.

Their names come up in conversation, they hear about opportunities first, they earn more and they have more fun doing it — they have made a name for themselves in their industry and the rewards show up in volumes.

If you do the things that impact your reputation in a positive way you will attract more opportunities. These opportunities create wealth and success.

There are five ways to position yourself as a "key person of influence" in your field:

- **Pitch.** Take the time to prepare how you answer the question "what do you do?" Choose for yourself a "micro-niche" and own that space rather than being another generalist. If you get into a conversation with someone, you must engage their imagination, be memorable, credible, clear and believable. People who have made a name for themselves are very clear on how they add value and they can explain it to others.
- **Publish.** Write down your key ideas, create articles, blogs and even a book about what you do. With few exceptions, it's nearly impossible to make a name for yourself if you aren't publishing your ideas somewhere.
- **Products.** You will get known by the products you create or associate yourself with. Make sure you only align to products and services that are an authentic expression of who you are and you feel proud to be associated with them.
- **Profile.** Raise your profile online and in the media. Make sure you dominate the front page of Google when

someone searches for you. Get featured in the press and post it online. If search engines like Google can't find you, your reputation is in serious trouble.

- **Partnerships.** You don't have enough time in the day to do everything yourself. If you put your time into creating a brilliant product, partner with someone who has wide-reaching distribution. If you have a great brand, partner with someone who has highly developed products. Network, connect and partner with the key people in your industry.

Never has there been a better time in history to make a name for yourself. New technology and the widespread sharing of resources make it easier than ever to do all five of the steps listed above.

No need to look for some special secret to wealth. The secret is: you are already standing on a mountain of value but you need to let the world know about it. After you've made a name for yourself, expect to see more opportunity, more fun, more inbound enquiries and even a lot more money.

If you put more focus into building your reputation, enhancing your brand and making a name for yourself in your industry, you'll always have a valuable asset.

It can take 20 years to build a reputation
and 5 minutes to ruin it.
If you think about that,
you'll do things differently.
Warren Buffet

THE THIRD KEY: VITALITY

Coming from a space of vitality rather than functionality is a characteristic at the heart of every great leader, adventurer, author, actor or entrepreneur.

Functionality is defined as performing a set of tasks or processes efficiently. It's a given that you need to be proficient at what you do. However, it just won't get you closer to success in the Entrepreneur Revolution.

There are two literal definitions of the word "vital" – the first is "irreplaceable" and the second is "life-force."

Money, wealth, power and influence move towards people who are the "irreplaceable life-force" in their domain.

The people who aren't easy to get rid of, the ones who can't be forgotten; these are the people who truly make it.

There are countless books and seminars available today that focus on automating and systemizing what you do. They tell you to avoid putting your personality into your business because you will get stuck in the business.

They say you shouldn't get too known in your field or else people will want to deal with you personally. They say you should build the business so it doesn't need you.

I don't agree with this approach in its entirety.

I agree that you should not be doing functional tasks that could be automated or systemized. However, I believe the purpose of getting these tasks taken care of is so you can become even more vital to your business.

Your goal is to move to higher and greater levels of irreplaceability.

People who are functional end up being replaced; people who are vital end up with ownership. They stay true to their centre and they own their space. Often, this results in them owning their marketplace, their business and their niche too.

Vital people have a sense of curiosity, a spark, a contagious energy and a genuine desire to serve at a new, higher standard.

Recently, I watched a documentary about the legendary hair stylist, Vidal Sassoon. Everyone he met described him as a true artist. He cared about hair; he wasn't satisfied unless he gave it his all.

He studied architecture for inspiration. He danced around the person in the chair as he styled them. You could never tell him the haircut you wanted. Instead he would study your face and tell you what haircut he would do for you.

Vidal Sassoon became a very, very rich man. He didn't try to retire from hairdressing, he tried to find ways to impact even more people and to get into it deeper than anyone else. He was vital.

My friend Cathy Burke is the CEO of the Hunger Project Australia. She brings so much life to that organization that people can't help but get involved. Under her commitment it's gone from annual revenues of a few hundred thousand dollars into the millions; and it's still climbing.

She has put in place lots of systems and best-practices but only for one reason; she wants all the boring stuff taken care of so her team can spend more time and energy being engaged with the cause.

Great entrepreneurs don't use systems, technology and best practices to get out of their business. They use them to get in deeper.

Vital people don't dream of retiring some day. In fact, they think about ways that they can keep doing more of what they love to do for as long as they can.

Rupert Murdoch is a billionaire and he is in his 80s; he hasn't retired yet. Warren Buffet is the second richest guy in the world; he's also in his 80s and he hasn't retired either.

I could make a list of almost every billionaire in the world who is in "retirement age" and almost every single one of them still shows up to work!

But, of course, it isn't work. When it feels like work you want to retire, you want to knock off early, you need other hobbies to keep you sane and you are dreaming of going on holidays.

What you are actually dreaming of is being in a space of vitality. You are dreaming of what it would be like to wake up excited about what the day could offer you and doing things that make you feel even more invigorated than when you started. You yearn to be the life force.

Well, here is the amazingly good news. You live in a world where you have vast options and can do almost anything your heart desires!

You can create things, you can be a public speaker, you can trade things, you can invent things, you can bring people together; and any of that stuff could make you wealthy and fulfil your dreams.

Before you read on, do you agree or not? Every day, isn't the world showing you fresh new examples of people who are fully embracing life and making millions?

Are you seeing examples of people who hate their boring, replaceable life but at least they get paid fortunes? I'm not. I only see people who are leaning into their lives and getting the real rewards.

The truth about retirement is that you will dream about the days you were most engaged in life's meaningful work, or you will wish you had been.

Talk to any elderly person and they will tell you to quit trying to do something you hate for the money. They will tell you to go out and do something that inspires you while you still have time to do something great.

If you were in a vital space when you were creating your income wouldn't you certainly make more income? People would notice you more and want to do business with you more. It's time to give up on the dream of "passive income," "easy wins" and a "comfortable retirement." It's time to say:

"I will only do things I never want to retire from and I will do these things in a way that adds value to others and tangibly rewards me as well."

Wealth flows to vital people, not functional people. Wealth flows to people who build a reputation and a profile. Wealth flows to people who acknowledge their luck and go out to create more of it.

When you are ready for the next steps to becoming more vital, known and lucky please turn the page. We're about to turn your passion into a meaningful, profitable empire that helps other people.

Part II

Finding Your Place in the Entrepreneur Revolution

CHAPTER 8

THE ENTREPRENEUR SWEET SPOT

In these exciting times we're living in, for the first time in history, it's easy to make an income from almost anything you want.

In the Entrepreneur Revolution you can pursue a passion and live well from it. You can access a global market and enough people around the world can join in to make it a business.

For the first time in history, people can move into what I call the "entrepreneur sweet spot."

You only have to figure out three key ingredients and you will find that you wake up each day living very happily in the age of the Entrepreneur Revolution.

Here are the three ingredients you need to hit the entrepreneur sweet spot:

1. Do something you're passionate about.
2. Do something you're good at.
3. Do something that makes money.

Let's address these aspects one at a time.

1. DOING SOMETHING YOU ARE PASSIONATE ABOUT

Knowing your passion is very important for several reasons.

First, you need passion because you need to keep yourself engaged in the projects you are creating.

We live in the age of opportunity. It's not fair on your brain to give it so many things to choose from. Just 60 years ago, people hardly had any choices to make by comparison.

Your parents or grandparents had a peer-group of maybe 50–100 people. There were just a few restaurants in town. There were a few movies that came out each year. There were only two brands of most products to choose from, eight radio stations to listen to, four TV channels to watch, five newspapers to read. The previous generation had instructions on how to have a good life. They were told to "Work hard, get a good job, work hard, buy a house, work hard, pay your mortgage, work hard, retire, take a cruise, play golf, pass away with dignity."

Life must have been a lot simpler for them. For us, it's complex. There is an almost infinite number of opportunities coming at us every day – go on this holiday, buy this fragrance, upgrade to this phone, take this course, do these exercises, invest in these assets, give to this charity, read this blog, subscribe to this YouTube channel, accept this friend request, listen to this guru, follow this person's tweets.

How on earth are we supposed to live like this? Technology was meant to make our lives better, not make us go insane.

The answer is, you must develop your own personal compass. An understanding of your passion gives you this compass. You must take a deep, introspective look at what you want to do with your life and decide in advance what constitutes a good opportunity and what doesn't.

Without knowing what it is that you are passionate about, you will constantly be distracted by the infinite number of choices that bombard you every day.

Secondly, having a clear passion that others can tune into is a huge competitive advantage. I would go so far as to say, in the Entrepreneur Revolution it's nearly impossible to build a business without passion. You will always be beaten by the person who has it.

Remember, in the times we live in, you are in competition with people from all over the world. A dispassionate person can lose their opportunities to a passionate person who lives on the other side of the world.

DISCOVERING YOUR PASSION

Passionate people have a huge advantage over dispassionate people. A passionate person attracts opportunities like a magnet.

Vidal Sassoon was the world's highest paid hairdresser ever, he built an empire on his passion. Here's how he describes his job:

> *How fortuitous to be able to touch the human frame. To be exhilarated by a craft that constantly changes; to hold that substance growing from a human form that moulds, creates spontaneous fashion. To be involved in the poetry of change.*

Apparently, he's talking about cutting hair! He could only speak this way out of a genuine love of his craft.

Many people struggle with the big question "what's my purpose?" or "what should I do that I'm passionate about?"

It might seem like a big question, but it's actually not that hard to discover if you know the right questions to ask so you can tune into the passion that's already present.

After discussing this topic with hundreds of entrepreneurs I fully believe that your whole life has already been playing out a theme. Whether you are conscious of it or not, there's an underlying theme that's been showing up in your life since you were a child.

For me, the theme is entrepreneurship, personal em-powerment and fundraising for charity. For as long as I can remember, the big moments in my life revolved around these themes.

At age 10, I was running garage sales from my parents' house. I wouldn't just sell our families unwanted items, I would sell the neighbours' stuff on consignment as well!

As a kid, I was washing cars and pulling weeds to raise money for my Scout hall.

I also developed a love of personal development from a very young age. Before the age of 13, I was reading books about goal setting and comfort zones.

At the intersection of these themes I find myself incredibly passionate even to this day.

Today I have businesses in three countries. I raise a lot of money for charity through business and I'm still fascinated about what makes people able to perform at their best.

When someone offers me an opportunity, I simply need to decide if it fits with these themes of empowering people through entrepreneurship.

Your life also has a theme. There are things you've been doing almost your whole life that you keep coming back to. The trick is to discover what that theme is.

At first, most people tell me that their history contains many unrelated activities. After probing deeply with hundreds of people on this topic I know this isn't the case. I know that all the things that genuinely excite a person are somehow connected.

Richard Branson has 150 companies in the Virgin Empire. At first glance it would seem that they are all unrelated; what does an airline have to do with credit cards or mobile phones?

Probe a little deeper and you'll see that there's a theme. Richard Branson loves to shake up stale old industries and make them fun. He did it with magazines, music stores, airlines and banks – along with dozens of other industries that took themselves too seriously. If he sticks to the theme, he's happy and his businesses work.

I describe it like an apple tree. There might be lots of separate apples on the tree, but there's just one tree that keeps growing them. Likewise, there might be a lot of opportunities that interest you, but there's one key theme that links them together.

To get more apples, you need a big, strong apple tree. To get more of the right opportunities you need to understand what your theme is.

> To see Daniel talk about discovering your passion visit:
> www.entrevo.com/talk-passion

ACTIVITY: DISCOVER YOUR "THEME"

Your "theme" will take the form of a rant that begins with any of these four sentences.

1. "For as long as I can remember I've felt there's something exciting at the intersection of ... & ..."
2. "I deeply believe that the world needs ..."
3. "Never in history has there been a better time for ..."
4. "My whole life I've been fascinated by what happens when you mix ... & ..."

This rant will light you up and excite you. It will feel like a rant that's been waiting to emerge since you were very young. It will feel a bit like a crusade you want to embark on and you don't really care how it happens as long as it unfolds.

This rant is not commercial. It's not "I believe there needs to be another accountant in London."

My rant goes like this ...

"I believe there's great power at the intersection of entrepreneurship and human empowerment. There's an Entrepreneur Revolution that needs to take place. Billions of people need to discover their hidden entrepreneur and then use it as a vehicle to reclaim their power – economically, intellectually, emotionally and spiritually. I believe that an entrepreneurial population is an empowered population and that entrepreneurs, by nature, want to fix the problems that humanity faces. I believe that by creating millions more empowered entrepreneurial teams we will transform the planet and create a world that works for more people."

I could rant like that for hours. None of it is commercial, it's just the crusade I've been on for as long as I can remember. In the early days I didn't have the words to describe it but I just knew this is what I wanted to see happen in the world.

When your passion tree has deep roots under the surface it can grow big above ground.

2. DOING SOMETHING YOU'RE GOOD AT

Now that we've talked about discovering what you are passionate about, let's talk about the next step in moving to the entrepreneur sweet spot.

You can't just be passionate, you also need to deliver real value.

At the heart of every great business is something of value, an asset. You cannot build a business if there's a lack of value.

No matter how good your sales people are, no matter how much advertising you do, no matter how much you push, if there's no value there's no business in the long run.

I am fortunate enough to be mentored by some brilliant people. One of these people is a guy who used to be a top performing fund manager for a huge investment bank. Over lunch one day he said a sentence to me that changed my life.

He said: *"Income follows assets."*

If you want rental income you first need an asset called a house. He explained, all things being equal, a five-bedroom house earns more than a two-bedroom house. In fact, no amount of marketing and sales efforts can get a two-bedroom house to earn more than its five-bedroom counterpart.

You could make millions worth of sales next month if I gave you an exclusive contract to sell the Empire State Building.

When there's an asset, there are many ways to make money from it. If you want more income in your business you need a bigger asset.

In business the main asset you have is called "Intellectual Property," or "IP" for short.

I'm not necessarily talking about the legal definition of IP that has been formalized with trademarks, patents, etc. I'm talking about the *special stuff* that makes you valuable.

For now, IP represents your method of doing something, your unique philosophy behind what you do, the recipes for success that you know. It's your brand or reputation, it's your way of creating a culture that attracts top people.

All of these things are infused with magical stuff called IP.

So how do you create more of it? How do you know what IP you already have but take for granted? How do you dig up this gold?

You write.

You write articles, you write books, you write brochures, you draw diagrams and you get what's in your head out on paper (or onto a hard drive at least).

Most of the IP you have goes swirling through your brain so fast that you call it "intuitive." What you will discover is that it's often not intuitive. It's a thought process that happens really quickly.

Only when you sit down and write about what you do will you be able to slow it down enough to see what's really going on.

Whenever I have an idea, my first step is to write about it. I will write a blog or create a brochure for it. In doing so, I need to pin the idea down and make sure there's real value in it. When I see the blog or the brochure it either feels real or it becomes obvious how many ingredients are missing.

I also write case studies about clients we've helped. It makes me slow down and deconstruct the elements that were behind the success story.

In writing this book, I've become much clearer on many aspects of my personal philosophy, my methods and my value. I've talked a lot about these ideas but something magic happens when you have to write.

The content that you write will be used to make products, marketing materials, employee handbooks, investor memorandums and websites.

People will read what you write and decide if they want to spend time with you, buy from you, partner with you and even invest in you. Rarely can people make the decision to do any of that unless they read something. Certainly, it's hard to scale your business without great written content.

If you've never written much before, don't worry. You aren't trying to win a literary award; you're trying to slow down your mind and access valuable ideas.

Here's a list of things to write about your area of interest:

- Seven mistakes people make while trying to achieve a result.
- Five valuable ideas more people should be aware of.
- Ten maxims to live by.
- Five things that stop people implementing good ideas.
- Three case studies of success stories.
- A brochure for your core product.
- A white paper or special report.
- A book.

Trust the process. Sit down and write your ideas down. You will discover that you are standing on mountains of value that you just take for granted.

When you examine successful people, a very common trait is that they write. They keep journals, they publish articles and white papers. They are often authors of books.

This isn't just for the people reading it; it's for the author too. They develop valuable IP as a result of the writing process.

The next step is commercializing your ideas. If you want to make real money from your intellectual property, read on.

3. DOING SOMETHING THAT MAKES MONEY

The third step to living in the entrepreneur sweet spot is to learn how to earn money from what you are passionate about and how you can deliver value to others by doing it.

There's been extensive research into the link between money and happiness. Statistically, money does make you happier. Up to a point.

When you deliver value to others, you must be rewarded for it or you will eventually become resentful.

The amount of money you need to earn may vary from person to person. However, one survey I found in the USA said $80,000 per year per person was a significant number for maximizing happiness. In the study, more money consistently equalled more happiness up to $80,000 per year but, after that threshold, more money had very little impact on happiness at all. Some people earning a lot more money became unhappy because of all the stresses that come with it.

For you it might be more or it might be less than other people. However, I could almost guarantee it's less than you think.

The mainstream media has us convinced that people need to be making millions to be fulfilled. After a while we think that happiness requires six cars, four houses, a treasure chest full of jewellry and endless travel.

Supposedly, we're meant to make all this money while we sleep and doing something that causes no stress.

As a result of this fantasy, I regularly see people who write down goals of millions (sometimes even billions) as their financial targets. This is a surefire recipe to be incredibly disappointed for the rest of your life!

You need a lot less than that to be happy.

A 2011 study into the UK economy found the average income was £26,000. In London (supposedly one of the wealthiest cities on earth) the average income is still less than £30,000 per year. This means the city, as a whole, is designed to function for people who earn about £30k. Anyone earning more than £30k has it better financially than most people in London. Anyone earning less than £30,000 is finding it tougher.

Believe it or not, in London the top 10% of income earners simply earned more than £60,000 in 2011.

I've discovered most people are very happy if they can earn about double the average wage for their city. After that amount, making more money often creates more stress for them than it's worth.

There's a small (tiny actually) number of people who truly love business for its own sake. They genuinely love building teams, juggling finances, raising capital, launching products and everything else that goes with a bigger business. These people can earn a lot more money than most and still be happy because they love business.

For most people, however, you don't need to build a massive business and earn millions. You can build a lifestyle business that generates a healthy six-figure revenue, by doing what you are passionate about. That allows you to take home a healthy income while still having a great deal of freedom and lifestyle.

In the next chapter, I'm going to give you a formula for building that sort of business.

CHAPTER 9

BUILDING A GLOBAL SMALL BUSINESS IN THE ENTREPRENEUR REVOLUTION

A business isn't about desks, computers, business cards, staff, accounting software or websites.

You are in business to develop and commercialize IP.

That's it.

How that happens takes many forms but, at the guts of it, you're creating or sourcing products and then making money from them.

The ideas in this section are powerful. I've used these ideas to create five start-ups; each went from $0 to $1 million in sales in under a year. It's these ideas that made me a millionaire by age 30.

I've also used these ideas with my clients and seen radical and dramatic increases in revenue and profit.

Provided you have value, we can use the following process to maximize the amount of money you can make from it.

PRODUCT STRATEGY: THE KEY TO MAKING MONEY FROM YOUR IDEA

At the heart of every business is a product. If you have a product, you can begin to build a business.

I have a strange definition of product.

I define a product as a consistent way of achieving a desired outcome that your customer wants.

When I look at a Rolex, I don't see the product as being a watch. I see the product as "a conspicuous device that communicates status and high achievement."

A person who buys a Rolex does not want to buy a device that tells the time. They could buy a $20 Casio that does a better job of telling the time. The desired outcome the customer wants to achieve has more to do with what a Rolex says about the wearer.

If the management at Rolex thought they were in the watch business, they would miss the point of what "product" they are really selling.

When you think about your product, you need to be very clear about the real problem you are solving. You need to see yourself as someone who is project managing some sort of result for your clients.

If you have a service, you need to structure it in a highly repeatable way so it begins to resemble a product. You should also give your services a special name, like you would a product.

Imagine two accountants. The first one thinks of himself as offering a service: "tax advice and compliance." The second one sees herself as a product creator. She has three products: "Fixing Financial Mess," "Small Business Growth Plan" and "Exit for the Max." Which accountant would you rather talk to? Who would earn money and have a business that scales?

The first key to commercializing your business is deciding what product you are actually selling and giving it a name that best reflects the customer need you solve (as an interesting side note, the name "Rolex" was a made-up word that the founder thought sounded luxurious in any language). This simple decision will largely impact how much money you make for the life of the business.

The next step is choosing how you will take it to market. I am going to recommend that you use a very special product strategy that I have developed called an Ascending Transaction Model (ATM).

In order to understand why this strategy works I need first to share several strategies that don't work.

PRODUCT STRATEGIES THAT DON'T WORK FOR SMALL BUSINESS

I've worked with thousands of small business owners over the last ten years who have come in contact with my training businesses.

What I have noticed is that many of them have a flawed product strategy. From day one, I can tell they will fail simply by the way they are taking their product to market.

Let me share four common product strategies that don't work for small business.

1. ONLY ONE PRODUCT OR SERVICE (OOPS) – TOO BRAND DEPENDENT

This is where a business only has one product or service. You either take it or leave it.

When you ask the owner of an OOPS business what range of products they can sell you, they are likely to say things like: "I do plumbing, you can buy plumbing services from me." "I sell IT services, you can get me to help with your IT problems."

This is the most common strategy in a traditional small business; and the reason these businesses stay small. It can work if you build a massive brand behind that single product like Zippo lighters or Tabasco sauce did. In most cases, however, a small business rarely ever builds a big enough brand to make an OOPS business work.

2. J CURVE — TOO CAPITAL DEPENDENT

This is by far the most common and most dangerous business model that people lose money on.

The "J curve" describes a business that predictably needs a lot of money invested before it makes a profit.

Typically, this kind of business requires huge sales volumes in order to cover its basic overheads. If you have a slow month, chances are you will lose a lot of money.

Most "J curve" businesses don't make money for 3–5 years. However, if they make it through the dip, they are very profitable and very valuable.

A typical small example is a restaurant. It costs lots of money to set up a new restaurant. There's the deposit, the leases, the fit out, the equipment, the stock, the marketing, the hiring and training of staff. The restaurant owner has to spend hundreds of thousands of dollars before the doors are even open.

Even after the doors are open, the running costs aren't small either. Each month a restaurant needs to sell thousands of meals before it covers its costs and makes money.

It can take months, or even years, to build up a loyal following of customers who make a restaurant profitable. If you don't have the capital to stay open, you will go broke before you get through the dip.

On the other end of the scale is a software company. Software businesses are typically "J curve" businesses. They invest millions of dollars into developing a product that will sell for $100 per unit.

What's worse is that people will often pirate their product and distribute it for free. If the business didn't raise enough money on day one, it's likely to run out of cash before it hits enough sales volume to cover its costs.

3. ONE-STOP SHOP – TOO SYSTEMS DEPENDENT

A one-stop shop is a business that tries to sell too many products, or tries to offer too much customization. Effectively, a customer comes in contact with the business and can make hundreds of product choices.

Amazon is a one-stop shop. Wal-Mart is too. These businesses offer thousands and thousands of product options.

The problem with this type of business is there are too many moving parts. Too many things can go wrong. It's too easy for your customers or staff to "break" the business.

In order to run this sort of business profitably, you need absolutely bulletproof systems. If you don't have the systems in place, you will always be pulling your hair out trying to fight fires.

I often see small businesses that are trying to sell hundreds of products but not getting any traction with any of them. The market doesn't see them standing out for anything and the business is always dealing with some drama that relates to one of its many products.

4. BROKERAGE MODEL - TOO TIME DEPENDENT

Brokerage businesses sell other people's value. The typical example is a real estate agency or a car yard. They don't own the assets they sell, they just go out and find a buyer.

My first businesses were all brokerage model businesses. I would go and find a product that I thought was going to be hot and I would take it to market.

Despite turning over millions, I was always shocked to discover that these early ventures were not worth real money to investors or acquirers.

Whenever I would get my business valued, I would be told the same thing "*you* are the business," or "there's no real asset in this business that you own." One person described my business as a "sales engine."

They would tell me that despite our team, our seven figure revenue and our offices, if we stopped working the business would grind to an immediate halt.

What I didn't have was Intellectual Property. It would be cheaper for someone to set up in competition with me than to buy my business.

Despite the downsides of this business model, it is by far the best way to start out in business.

If you've never been in business before, don't go out and invent your own products. Go and find someone who has a successful product and help them to sell more of it or help them to sell it in a new territory.

Two years working as a brokerage for someone else will teach you about business. You won't need to worry about product development, you will just need to get good at sales, marketing and administration. Vital skills for any entrepreneur.

If you broker someone else's product, your job is simply to find ways to sell it efficiently. This skill will be invaluable to you later in your business life.

A brokerage business won't really attract investors, it won't sell for much but it will teach you everything you need to know about running a successful business.

Once you have the basics down, you can then develop your own products in a way that does create real value.

CHAPTER 10

THE ASCENDING TRANSACTION MODEL (ATM)

Knowing what you are passionate about is not enough to make money in business. Having a valuable IP is not enough either. If you want to make money from your business you need to have an elegant product strategy.

In this chapter we're going to look at a very powerful product strategy that makes a lot of money. It involves four types of products that strategically work together to generate a lot of revenue.

I have called this system an Ascending Transaction Model (ATM) because I want you to remember that it's designed to give you money.

Great businesses have four types of products that all serve a unique purpose:

1. Gifts
2. Products for prospects (PFP)
3. Core offerings
4. Logical next steps (LNS)

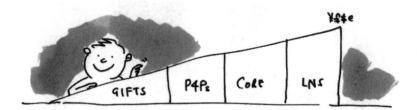

RULES FOR CREATING EACH PRODUCT IN THE ATM

Let's take a look at each of these types of products in order and place some rules around them to make sure they are doing their job.

1. GIFTS

Gifts are free products that you give to the world expecting nothing in return. You don't ask for contact details, you don't ask for money, you don't ask for anything. They are thoughtful, valuable and enticing in their own right and they show just how brilliant your business is.

A great gift is delightful if it's given to the right person at the right time. It needs to open people up to a whole new world of value that your business offers.

Your gift should entice people to want to know more about what you do and what value you offer.

Big companies like Rolex, Qantas, Credit Suisse and Kia give us the tennis, the golf, yacht races and other sporting events as a gift. They pay for these events to run and you don't have to be a customer to enjoy them.

Apple gives you iTunes for free. Google gives you browsers, calendars, maps, apps and more for free.

In a small business, a gift can be a DVD, a book, a YouTube channel full of great content, a downloadable checklist or a sample.

The key is that you give it freely and ask nothing back from the person who receives it.

RULES FOR CREATING A GIFT

1. **It is given as a gift without conditions.** The gift must be given freely, it must be perceived as valuable and timely. You must not ask for anything in return, you release the gift "free to the world."
2. **It must be meaningful.** A great gift can open people up to a whole new world; a world where the problems and frustrations they've had don't exist the way they used to.
3. **It doesn't send you broke.** The gift must be low cost for you to deliver; you can't go broke giving gifts. In most cases it will be a digital gift, social media or an event experience (all of these have a very low and manageable cost per person).

2. PRODUCTS FOR PROSPECTS

This is a product for people who want to try you out without committing too much money or time. This type of product is designed to offer a quick win or a first-hand experience. It's a sample of things to come, a test drive or a first step in the right direction.

A good law firm will offer a free first consultation, a car dealership might invite you to a special event, a small business might get you to buy a home study kit or attend a low-cost seminar.

Products for prospects need to have a low cost. Either a small amount of money, some focused time or sharing of contact details.

The product for prospects is designed to ignite the commercial relationship between your business and your ideal customer.

It should warm people up to doing business with you, share some of your philosophy, demonstrate your value and do it all quickly and cheaply.

Apple have the iPod Nano. BMW have branded clothing. Google offer an Adwords voucher. Accountants invite people to attend a networking event in their office.

Small businesses can run events or webinars, create memberships, offer downloads or have books or DVDs all very cheaply.

RULES FOR CREATING A PRODUCT FOR PROSPECTS

1. **Get your ideas out to the world.** The product for prospects should be focused on sharing your ideas and philosophies. Not generic ideas, not old ideas, not small ideas. Share your big, unique and transformational ideas with your prospects. Ideas are cheap these days – make your money on the implementation of the ideas.

2. **Get contact details.** A product for prospects should be exchanged for accurate contact information. It's OK to charge for this product if you like and it's also OK to give

it at no charge *but* you must get people's contact details in the process.

3. **Quick wins.** You want to make sure that people get some sort of quick benefit from this product, preferably in under seven days. If you charge, it should be priced cheaply enough that people feel they got a very good deal considering how quickly they started to see value. The product for prospects should lead people closer to the decision to buy your core product but not cannibalize your core product. A quick win doesn't mean that the problem is completely solved and there's no longer a need to do more with your business.

3. A CORE PRODUCT

These are the products (or services) you are famous for.

For BMW it's cars. KPMG's core offering is auditing. Singapore Airlines are known for long-haul flights.

With these products you can deliver a full and remarkable solution to what people want. These products seriously solve problems.

They are your main focus and your customers and clients can't stop talking about them. These products are priced to be profitable. It's OK to lose small money on gifts and products for prospects but not on your core business.

You've giving people a taste of what you can do with your product for prospects but now it's time to be paid for your fair value when someone wants to access your core business.

You must create a special methodology that makes your core offering remarkable. You need to push your team to be the best in your market for this type of product.

It's important that you develop enticing brochures and websites for your core product. You should raise your profile as the leader in your industry for your core product.

The key is to create a full and remarkable solution to your ideal customer's problem. You want your core product to turn people into evangelists for your brand.

RULES FOR CREATING A CORE PRODUCT

1. **A remarkable solution.** The core business must be a full and remarkable solution to a real problem your potential clients face. By definition, a remarkable product is something that is worth talking about. Your goal is to create your product in a way that people want to tell their friends how good it is.

2. **Implementation, not ideas.** In most cases your business will implement some sort of change for a customer or client. You will create something they couldn't create on their own or you will work with them closely to help them create it properly. Do not fall into the trap of thinking that you will make money just by sharing your ideas. We live in a world where people already have access to ideas free of charge; they don't have time to implement the ideas and they want to pay you big money to do it for them (or to get them to do it right). When someone has your core product they feel it solved a problem or created a huge benefit.

3. **The price is right.** The job of the core product is to make profit; you can break even or even lose small money on gifts and products for prospects but you must *never* undersell your core product at a loss or a break even.

The core business must cost more than £1000 per client per year. Every time a client says yes to doing business with your small business, it must generate an order of thousands of pounds minimum. You can't run a profitable business on small sales. It's OK to have a small unit cost, but the minimum order size must be £1000+ per year. If not, I would say it's a product for prospects *not* a core business sale.

4. A LOGICAL NEXT STEP (LNS)

Your core product was so delightful that your clients want to know what comes next. The LNS products are the products you mostly sell to people who've already bought your core business.

BMW are known for their cars but they make a lot of money in finance and insurance (the logical next step after you've just bought a car). Then they service your vehicle and eventually they handle the sale of your older car as they upgrade you to their new model.

Your LNS product should be highly profitable. Selling to existing clients is highly profitable because the cost of winning the relationship has already been covered.

The LNS product creates a long-term underpinning of your business. With this fourth product you should do well in business for many years to come.

RULES FOR CREATING A LOGICAL NEXT STEP

1. **It's highly profitable.** The logical next step should aim to double the profitability of your business. This product is

designed to be sold to existing clients so you don't have the huge costs of building a relationship with them. A well-selected second product should have the potential to double the profit in your business.

2. **It's different.** It must not simply be more of the same. If your core business is accounting, your LNS can't be more accounting in some other form; instead it could be legal services, business coaching, software, temping staff, etc.

3. **It's logical.** You don't want to confuse your clients with a second product offering that just doesn't fit with your brand. If you sell graphic design services, you don't want to offer personal training as a second sale because it just doesn't seem to make sense. The LNS product is a "logical next step" that shows up after you solved the first problem. For example, after a fitness trainer helps their client lose weight the client logically wants to buy new clothes; the fitness trainer could add a personal image consulting service to their business.

THESE PRODUCTS FIT TOGETHER IN A PRODUCT ECOSYSTEM

These four types of product are designed to string together and create a product ecosystem. They take a client on a journey from barely knowing your business to feeling great about doing a lot of business with you.

Your potential clients will appreciate a gift that is given in the spirit of being thoughtful.

They will then want to try out something without too much risk. They might be happy to spend a small amount of money for a quick win. Your product for prospects is the perfect thing for them to try you out.

After having two positive experiences with your business, a client may now be open to spending money on your core business. You can also bet they are the right kind of client because they now have a better understanding of you too.

If your core business is as good as you've said it is, your client will have other wants, needs or problems that they would like you to help them with. Your LNS product will be the perfect thing.

As I said, most of the costs in acquiring a client have already been absorbed in the previous products so you may discover that you end up earning more profit on the LNS product than in your core.

If you do it correctly, you will have constructed a seamless journey for your clients. They will enjoy dealing with you because they don't feel pressured or rushed to make a big decision; they feel each decision is quite natural and is based on positive past experiences with you and your business.

CREATING THE ECOSYSTEM THAT LINKS YOUR PRODUCTS

It's not enough simply to have these four types of products in your business. You need the glue that links them up to form an ecosystem.

There are three key pieces of "glue" that hold your ATM together.

1. LEAD CAPTURE PROCESS

You need to capture people's details. Prospective clients need to be able to signal to you that they are interested in doing business by registering their contact details with you.

This could be on your website (e.g. fill in your details and then download our research paper). It could also be a good old-fashioned fishbowl on the counter for people to put their business card in. It could be a form that gets filled in by your staff. It could be a "Facebook Connect" button that automatically connects your businesses page to your client. However you structure it, capturing people's contact details is a key part of your business and you should have several ways to collect them.

A lot of people who receive your gift product will want to engage with you. Make sure they can.

Start to become more aware of how other companies capture your details. You might be surprised to discover that you are handing over your details several times per week in various forms. Additionally, research the people in your industry and find out who is capturing details in a professional and brand-affirming way. Take these lead-capturing processes and put them into your business.

2. SALES CONVERSATIONS

The next piece of glue is sales. It's a very important part of every business that many small business owners often avoid.

Secretly, many small business owners have a negative association to selling and they wish they could simply do extra marketing, extra servicing or extra networking rather than having to have the sales conversation.

Unfortunately, this is a fantasy. Omega, Ferrari, Google, HSBC and Apple all invest in sales training so their staff know how to have a structured sales conversation with a prospective buyer.

If the world's biggest brands, with the world's hottest products, need to have sales conversations then so does every small business.

The good news is, if someone has had a good experience with your gift and products for prospects, the sales conversation will be an enjoyable experience. Products for prospects and gifts are brilliant for warming people up to be pre-sold before they meet you for a sales chat.

In many cases, a person who has experienced your product for prospects already suspects they want to do business with you but they just need to clarify some finer points and sort out the particulars.

I would go so far as to say that you (or your sales people) should avoid talking to people unless they have experienced a product for prospects. If someone calls out of the blue and wants to talk business, be sure to send them the gift or the product for prospects before you meet with them.

I recommend that you become more keenly interested in how sales conversations are structured. Go and put yourself in situations where you can be sold to, find out what works for you as a buyer and what doesn't. See if you can create the ultimate "buying experience" out of your sales conversations.

3. SERVICING PROCESS

The final piece of glue is service. Your clients need you to look after them *better* than you said you would.

This means you must strategically undersell your core product. You must keep some aces up your sleeve and resist the temptation to tell prospects about everything you will do for them once they are a client.

If you tell your prospects that you take your clients away each year on a river cruise, they will expect it. When the invite arrives they will think "He did what he said he was going to do."

If, for some reason, you didn't do the river cruise, your clients would feel they missed out on something you said you would do.

Conversely, if you are disciplined and you never mentioned the river cruise, when the invite arrives your client will likely feel special because you've done something above and beyond their expectations.

Even after you've delivered value to your clients, they will want to know that they are still valued and you're still available to them.

You must build into your business special ways to look after your existing clients, long after they have bought from you.

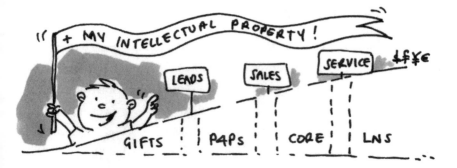

You can put them into an online club membership or forum, you can invite them to "clients only" events, you can send them updates. Make sure it's delightful though.

If you send out a half-hearted newsletter once a month it will have the opposite effect on your clients: rather than being delighted by you, they will be annoyed.

If people are delighted by your servicing, they will want to buy your LNS product. If you fail to service your existing clients, no matter how good your core product is, it's unlikely you will get an uptake on your next offering.

Think of all the businesses you have bought from in the last year or two. See if you can think of who has looked after you as a client above and beyond your expectations.

Can you recall special events, little surprises or unexpected value that showed up after you were already a client? If not, can you imagine what you would have loved them to do? When you have some ideas, design some surprises for your existing clients.

THE COMPLETE ATM

Now you have the four products and you have three pieces of glue that form a product ecosystem. When you put them in order, you end up with an Ascending Transaction Model.

You will create a nice, easy way for people to do business with you at several levels. People will love being around your business and they will feel good about buying from you several times.

The best part of an ATM is that you can simply go around making sure people get given gifts and products for prospects. After that, the domino effect kicks in and you have a business that just flows.

WHAT HAPPENS WHEN YOU DON'T HAVE A PRODUCT ECOSYSTEM?

It takes time to create an ATM. You put many hours into strategy, design and production in order to get it right.

Failing to do so, however, shouldn't be an option.

Many small business people want their business to be easy and simple so they just don't bother to put together an ATM.

With too few products, they make the error of pushing their core business too soon. They expect people who hardly know them to open their wallet and start spending.

When this doesn't happen, the business owner makes the mistake of lowering the price of the core business to a level that isn't profitable and they begin to resent their business and their clients.

If they don't lower the price, too few potential customers make the leap. They might be charging a fair price but simply don't have enough clients to run the business.

The issue isn't the price of the core product; the issue is that the business has not created a relationship; something the gift and product for prospects are designed to do.

Even if the business has these first three products it will be profitable. However, without the LNS, the business is probably doing barely half the profit it is capable of.

An Ascending Transaction Model covers your bases. It has products that build relationships and products that deliver value. It gets you out to market and it makes you money.

The key is taking time to carefully plan and produce the products you will have in your ATM. If you simply give up, you're destined to stay small and struggle to make money from your venture.

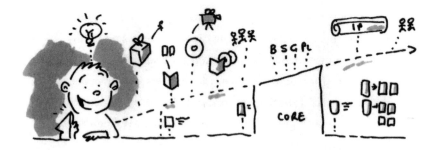

A BIG LESSON OR BIG RESULT

Not only have I used the ATM strategy to grow several multi-million dollar businesses myself, I've used this formula with hundreds of my clients and it's staggering how fast their businesses become dramatically more profitable.

I've seen a personal trainer go from £50k a year to £200k a year in one year. I've seen a consultant go from £80k a year to £500k in just 20 months after implementing an ATM. I've seen a charity go from $2.5m a year in donations to $4m the following year using this strategy.

I've seen it work with all sorts of businesses and charities.

When you put the ATM into your business one of two things will happen very quickly.

1. Either you will get a big result and start seeing your business succeed.
2. Or you will discover that your business idea is lacking something very fundamental and you need to make a big change.

Unfortunately, until you have an elegant business model like the Ascending Transaction Model, you simply won't know.

It's easy to blame the economy, the competition, the government, the clients or the staff. If your business is under-performing, I urge you not to blame any external factor until after you've implemented an ATM strategy with excellence. After that, you can go looking for another reason.

Maybe your idea is great or maybe it sucks; it's impossible to tell unless you've tested out how that product fits with your ATM.

A single product out on its own won't tell you much. It might be an amazing core offering but, without a product for prospects helping it along, it might not sell.

You might have a created a great product for prospects, but you just don't have a remarkable core offering to back it up.

It's important to know the Ascending Transaction Model isn't an overnight phenomenon. It's a powerful strategy but it can take time to implement.

You need to create products that you are proud of. My clients often take between 6 and 12 months to get their ATM just right. Many discover on day one that they don't have a core offering and they have been trying to rest their business upon a product for prospects.

This is a good framework but it's not valuable until it becomes more than just an idea.

In the next part of this book, I'm going to focus on overcoming the roadblocks to implementation. I want to discuss what's required for you to go from a good idea to an exceptional business.

In the chapter ahead, you'll discover what you must focus on in order to be successful as an entrepreneur and make the most of the times we are living in.

To see Daniel talk about the Ascending Transaction Model visit:

www.entrevo.com/talk-atm

PART III

LIVING THE ENTREPRENEUR REVOLUTION DREAM

CHAPTER 11

THE SEVEN-STAGE JOURNEY INTO THE ENTREPRENEUR REVOLUTION

There is a predictable journey you are going to go on as you leave the industrial age and enter the Entrepreneur Revolution.

Without knowing this predictable journey you may get frustrated at times. Maybe things seem like they aren't moving fast enough, or maybe too fast. Maybe you try to run before you can crawl and end up falling down again and again. Maybe you find yourself on a plateau without a clear path to go to the next level.

Without a clear journey you won't make the best of these times you are living in. For that reason, I've mapped out what I consider to be the predictable path you are likely to take as you fully embrace the Entrepreneur Revolution.

The first part of the journey is "work." It feels like work and it's where most of us get started.

Work wasn't designed to make you wealthy or fulfilled. It was designed to make you enough money and grant you enough satisfaction that you don't cause a problem for your employer or for society. Work is the comfy little treadmill that you are expected to run on to keep the industrialized society functioning.

Today, the purpose of work is to discover what you love, to get experience and to meet other people in your field. It still isn't designed to make you wealthy but it's there to lay the foundations.

THE THREE LEVELS OF "WORK"

LEVEL 1: THE NEWBIE

The newbie is fresh, new and enthusiastic in a particular vocation or role. Their job is to learn the ropes and become functional. Often a newbie is called an apprentice. Everyone must do their time as an apprentice. If you are lucky, you will do an apprenticeship under a great mentor and you will set yourself up for a fast-track tour of the workforce. Most people, however, will simply do their training, become functional and then progress to the next level.

LEVEL 2: THE WORKER

After sufficient time in an apprentice role, you become functional and ready to be a worker. You can now do the things you were trained to do by your mentor and you can perform the tasks that will create value for someone who's organizing your labour. You might become ambitious in the workforce and seek out a new mentor who will help prepare you for higher levels of functionality.

You may even find yourself working your way up the job ladder and doing very important work. Most people in society never go beyond this level; they bounce between apprentice and worker their whole career, always staying in the comfort zone where they don't want to rock the boat. A small group of people have an entrepreneurial seizure and decide they should work for themselves at the next level.

LEVEL 3: SELF-EMPLOYED

Self-employment might seem like a big, exciting change for a worker. However, little do they realize, they lack some crucial ingredients as an entrepreneur. As a worker, they were trained to believe that value is all about functionality.

The more functional you are the more valuable you are.

Subconsciously, they take these beliefs into their own enterprise and create even more work for themselves. As a worker, they had regular pay, support and didn't need to worry how the whole organization performed. Now they have their old job to do plus a ton of other jobs that they never really considered until after they were self-employed. They find themselves having to make sales, compile accounts, fix IT problems, manage workflow, come up with strategies and even make the coffee too.

The three levels we've just looked at make up the vast bulk of society. Only a tiny fraction of people are able to move beyond the worker levels into the realms of being an entrepreneur who gets to "play." Moving into the "play" category is how you begin living in the Entrepreneur Revolution.

THE THREE LEVELS OF "PLAY"

LEVEL 4: KEY PERSON OF INFLUENCE

When a self-employed person ceases to see themselves as functional and starts seeing themselves as vital they become a "key person of influence." In every industry, there are a group of key people whose names come up in conversation, who attract opportunities and who make a lot of money while having fun. Becoming a key person of influence is what's required to break the feeling of work and functionality. It's the first step into the Entrepreneur Revolution.

Key people of influence are clear about their vision, they are credible and they are able to attract resources. They easily attract a team, they can get investors excited, they have more customers than they know how to supply. Best of all, they begin to have fun again!

LEVEL 5: CAMPAIGN-DRIVEN ENTERPRISE

Key people of influence eventually attract opportunities allowing them to tap into larger distribution, leverage on established brands and to align themselves with attractive products.

The fastest way to begin to monetize these sorts of opportunities is with something I call a "campaign-driven enterprise" (CDE). It's a business that creates a series of exciting promotions, events and launches in order to make the most of the opportunities that seem to keep showing up.

CDEs can make huge amounts of money in the Entrepreneur Revolution. However, they also have a downside. When you take your foot off the accelerator pedal, they slow down very rapidly. The month you stop promoting or launching something you see a sharp decline in your revenues and profits. For this reason, a savvy entrepreneur will move to the next level in the Entrepreneur Revolution.

LEVEL 6: THE GLOBAL SMALL BUSINESS

The global small business (GSB) is the ultimate goal of most entrepreneurs. It's a small- to medium-sized business, often with less than 150 people, and it seriously punches above its weight.

It's not linked to geography, it defines itself by an ideology or a philosophy. For that reason, it can trade anywhere and with anyone who shares a similar outlook.

It has a well-developed brand within a niche, a bulletproof sales and marketing engine, well-designed systems that automate functional tasks and a dynamic culture that entices high performers to want to stay.

A global small business will not slow down easily, it takes on a life of its own and the challenge is not how to grow it, the challenge is how to direct it as it expands so that it doesn't explode.

As the creator of a global small business you will need to become good at saying no to things that aren't exactly right for your brand. GSBs get opportunities flooding in and if you say yes to too many of them, your GSB will collapse. Like a race car driver, you must stay intensely focused on the path ahead and not go thinking about the side streets that might be nice to explore.

Most people would be thrilled to reach this level. As the owner of a GSB you will be known by your peers, you will be affluent, well-travelled and spend most of your time doing things that matter to you. Only after you reach this stage will you fully appreciate why you need to go one step further and why you also had to wait until now to achieve the final level.

There is a final bonus level in the Entrepreneur Revolution where you get to really play a big game.

THE BONUS LEVEL!
LEVEL 7: MAKING A DIFFERENCE ENTERPRISE (MADE)

After building a GSB you will discover that you have influence, money, time and a well-developed sense of purpose and character. You will not be able to resist the thought of leaving a positive legacy and doing something that is meaningful and lasting. You will want to have an impact through your business directly or through politics, the media or your wealth and influence.

After building a GSB you will have the skills, contacts and resources to really do this. Had you attempted it too soon, you would not have been able to do this in a way that felt like your life's purpose. Probably, you would have turned your passion for making a difference into another job.

It would have become functional work and you would end up resenting the very cause you wanted to love. I meet people all the time who try to skip straight to this step out of a deep desire for altruism. They rarely succeed; they end up bitter that they gave so much but barely made a splash.

Even the well-known change makers went through similar steps to the ones I've outlined here. They started as apprentices to other change makers, they did the work, they became key people of influence, they launched their organizations, built a brand and a team and then finally got recognized for making a difference.

When you evolve to a MADE you don't have to sacrifice your own life. People who successfully create a MADE end up having more travel, more fun, more influence, more experiences, more fulfilment and, in many cases, even more money.

As an active entrepreneur who is making a difference, your GSB will benefit enormously.

Richard Branson's businesses are affected positively by the work of his charity Virgin Unite. Microsoft is benefited by the work of the Bill and Melinda Gates Foundation.

> To see Daniel talk about the 7 levels visit:
> www.entrevo.com/talk-seven-levels

Don't skip the levels

Each level is an important part of the journey. As much as you want to get to the higher levels, you will actually move faster towards your goal if you focus on advancing one level at a time.

Yes, this even includes being an apprentice and doing the work so that you understand the functionality of your industry. You don't have to stay at each level for years, or decades, like most people do – but you do need to stamp your foot clearly on the base before moving to the next one.

Remember to keep your eye on the prize. You're living in the most exciting time in history.

There's a renaissance unfolding. The whole world is evolving and reorganizing. This is the time for you to make a journey from an industrialized worker to an empowered entrepreneur.

This journey is worth it. As you make the crossing, you will discover yourself becoming a more evolved person capable of deeper thought, heightened empathy and more inspired decision-making abilities.

You will be capable of achieving the things that, just a few years ago, you thought of as dreams.

DO YOU HAVE WHAT IT TAKES?

Moving through these seven levels requires a certain attitude. Most people will go through their entire life working in a job feeling powerless to take charge of their own destiny. If you're going to be different, you'd better be ready for the challenges that come before the glory. So don't even embark on the journey of entrepreneurship unless you have the following three ingredients.

1. WILLINGNESS TO STRETCH

The very fact that you wish to create something new (a new lifestyle, a new product, a new business, a new result) means that you need to accept that it doesn't currently exist within your sphere of influence. If it did, you wouldn't be creating it. If you're creating something new, don't be shocked when it requires you to stretch.

Creating something worthwhile means that it will probably require more money than is in your current bank account, it will require more time than you have spare and it will require you to perform at a level you don't currently know how to. This means you're going to have to get used to being stretched.

You need to embrace the feeling of being stretched. Every time you feel that you're being pulled into the unknown, or there's too much to do, you need to smile and remember that this is what it feels like to be doing something big and meaningful.

Remember that you're the one who chose this journey and you knew it was going to require you to stretch. If you're stretched then it means things are working out the way you planned!

2. WILLINGNESS TO GET RESOURCEFUL

The way you deal with being stretched is to get resourceful. Rather than dwelling in the discomfort of how you are being stretched, you get proactive about finding a solution.

Being resourceful requires you to keep coming back to the fact that we live in a time where there's more money on the planet, more talented people on the planet and more access to great ideas than ever before in history. These resources already exist; you need only to go get them.

No amount of emotional frustration will help you get these resources; you don't get what you throw a tantrum for, you get what you *pitch* for.

If every time you get asked "how are you?" you respond by saying "there's no money, there's no time, there are no good people" you will "pitch it into existence."

The person listening will not respond by saying "let me solve all your problems for you." They will politely agree with you and reaffirm your view. Even if they have time, money or talent they will withhold it from you because they sense there could be good reasons why others aren't giving you resources.

Imagine if you respond to the question with "I'm grateful that I have so many good opportunities showing up. I have opportunities for talented people to create real value. I also have opportunities where extra capital can be used to create valuable assets in my business."

That pitch will get more people interested in helping you and investing in you.

If you want something new, you have to go and pitch for it. If you want money, you must pitch for it. If you want a team you must pitch them. If you want customers, investors, partners, mentors or promoters you must go out and pitch them. You get what you pitch for; and you're always pitching.

Resourcefulness is all about having resourceful conversations that move you in the right direction. It's about pitching for the things you want until you get them.

It's about dwelling on possible solutions rather than the dead ends. Very few people care about your complaints; they are too busy doing their own thing. Most successful people believe that if you live in a developed economy you don't have much to complain about, you just need to get on with it.

Once you're in a resourceful state and you are having resourceful conversations, it's just a matter of sticking to the path. After you know what needs doing, you must be willing to be held accountable for getting the results.

3. WILLINGNESS TO BE HELD ACCOUNTABLE

You will produce better results when you are held accountable. When you have deadlines to meet, you will do what needs to be done to hit them. When you have someone you respect pushing you to create your best work, you create your best work.

Most people know how to exercise and how to eat healthier meals. The reason we don't do it is because we don't have anyone else holding us to account.

Most people who get a fitness trainer suddenly start eating right and exercising every week because they have someone holding them to account, not because they have suddenly learned what to eat and how to exercise.

This principle applies to anything you want to do that requires you to stretch and to be resourceful. Anything that's complex and difficult can trigger your reptile brain's "escape and survive" mode. If your reptile "wakes up," your natural response will be to run and hide from the challenges.

Your monkey brain wants to do things that are mostly familiar with a pinch of drama thrown in. Your monkey brain isn't a great ally when it comes to stretching and getting resourceful. Your monkey brain is happier watching the TV, checking Facebook, answering emails or chatting with friends about their daily dramas.

At this time, you need an external motivational force to keep you on track. Your empire brain needs an ally so it can overthrow the monkey and the reptile.

The ally is external accountability. It needs someone else to help hold the original intention of creating something big, exciting and meaningful.

As you stretch, and as you get resourceful, you need external support to sustain you long enough to get results.

CHAPTER 12

THE SEVEN MAXIMS TO CULTIVATE A CULTURE OF RESULTS

If you have the three ingredients discussed in the previous chapter, you are ready to *begin* your journey and advance through the seven phases of the Entrepreneur Revolution.

Along the way you will encounter many difficult choices. Every entrepreneur's journey is complex and, without the right culture, you simply can't make the right decisions consistently.

The best way to cultivate this culture is through "maxims." In business, maxims are designed to be principles of high performance.

Maxims represent a core philosophy designed to inspire a way of being that produces the results you want.

Maxims are your compass. They are home truths, or principles, that help guide you through the complexity of building your empire from concept to multi-national operation.

Facebook has maxims like "move fast and break things" and "fail faster" to maintain its risk-taking, start-up culture.

Nike has maxims like "We're on the offensive always" and "It's in our nature to innovate" to keep them on track as a competitive sporting brand.

I am going to share with you the maxims of high performance that have helped guide me through the seven layers. These maxims have helped me to perform – despite recessions, setbacks and costly mistakes.

Attempt to adopt them as your own. When you are ready, I also encourage you to develop your own maxims that inspire you even more.

MAXIM 1: YOU GET WHAT YOU PITCH FOR ... AND YOU ARE ALWAYS PITCHING

A pitch is a powerful set of words that you deliver to the world again and again. Eventually, if you stick at it and really get the pitch perfected, you will get what you pitch for.

In your business, if you get your pitch right you can raise money, attract a team, engage partners and inspire new clients. If you are a change maker with a great pitch, you will eventually attract a following, upset the status quo and see a shift in your cause.

A client of mine, Lazo Freeman, began to pitch "I'm the UK's top body transformation coach, I work with wealthy men who are brilliant in a boardroom but ordinary in a bedroom and make them lean, fit and toned in 12 weeks." As a result, he has attracted very high-paying clients and he earns 500% more than he did when he simply pitched "I'm a fitness trainer."

Another example is my friend, Jeremy Gilley. In 1999 he began to pitch "I believe the world needs a day of peace which will serve humanity as a starting point for bringing us together despite our differences." By 2001, Jeremy found himself in the United Nations witnessing a unanimous resolution for a fixed calendar day of peace (September 21). He got what he pitched for; today over 100 million people celebrate Peace Day each year.

A powerful pitch, delivered hundreds of times, will allow you to speak your best ideas into reality; but it doesn't end there.

When you repetitively pitch a *bad* idea that doesn't help you it will have just as much power. If you are consistently pitching people "I have no money because, as a child, my parents complained about not having enough" you will also speak it into reality. People will begin to reinforce your belief, support you in making it real and reinforce its validity. You will get what you pitch for and you will have no money!

If you say "I'm overweight because of my age and because I have a slow metabolism," your pitch will start to work. You will have other people agree with you, you will start to see new reasons as to why this is absolutely true, you will have others feeding you research that spurs you on in your conviction. You will get what you pitched for and you will stay overweight!

When you consistently pitch an idea to people, it gains strength. Soon enough it becomes real to you and you can't see the world any other way.

So be careful what you pitch for. A pitch will bring you followers, believers, supporters, research and reinforcement no matter what you are pitching.

If you pitch "the world is miserable," more misery will start to show up. If you pitch "there's not enough," you will get scarcity. If you pitch "people aren't interested in my business," you will get more of that.

It is a choice. However, you get to choose what you want to pitch for. If you chosoe to pitch "life is good and I'm very lucky," you will get more of that too. If you pitch "there are clear opportunities in my life right now," you will start to see them.

Pitching is powerful, so be deliberate with your words because you will get what you pitch for and you are always pitching.

MAXIM 2: INFLUENCE COMES FROM OUTPUT ... NOT CONFIDENCE

Don't wait until you feel confident in your abilities before you create something. Confidence is not required.

Recently I watched a short video about influential people. It was beautifully shot but it didn't say very much. Just some very basic observations about people who have been influential in the past.

The opening line stated something that I flat out disagree with: "an influencer has a certain confidence that not many people have."

Take a look at Whitney Houston, Kurt Cobain, John Candy and Michael Jackson, and you won't see people who were supremely confident. You will see people who were perpetually tormented by their insecurities, plagued by self-doubt and a lack of confidence resulting in their own demise. Yet they were all massively influential.

Influence is not about confidence, influence is about output. You can lack confidence, you can be racked by self-doubt and you can secretly fear an imminent alien invasion *but* if you create amazing output you will gather influence.

Influencers are producers. We only know about influential people because of their prolific output.

They might have big houses and fancy things but that's not how they became influential. They create, not consume, for their influence.

The Beatles created the world's most valuable music catalogue in just eight years; they were prolific, not confident.

Stephen Spielberg has written over 20 screenplays, directed over 50 films and produced close to 200 movies; he's prolific, not confident.

Oprah Winfrey did 4561 episodes of her iconic talk show, she's written five books, published monthly magazines and produced daily radio shows; she's prolific, not confident.

Steve Jobs built three separate companies, was listed as the inventor on 317 patents, and is credited as reinventing seven industries; he was prolific, not confident.

It is creation that creates influence. It's your ability to write and publish, record and duplicate, design and produce. It's your ability to finish the job and put a completed product into the world.

The idea that influencers are simply cool, hip or trendy is superficial. It overlooks the enormous amounts of energy that influencers put into constantly reinventing their output.

It does not matter if you are confident or not. Produce something of value, create a product, publish a book, make a video, prototype a widget. If it's excellent output, you will gain influence.

I've worked with dozens of people on creating new things. Most of the people I've worked with had self-doubts to begin with, but we pushed to keep producing. Often the confidence came after the project was complete, but not before.

Logically, real confidence can only come *after* you have done something, not before. It may never come at all. Fear not, it doesn't matter, keep creating and your influence will go through the roof.

Don't let your perfectionism stand in the way either; prolific beats perfect too. Getting stuff done will create more momentum than waiting for everything to be perfect.

Creating all the time is fun and it generates all sorts of results. Wealth, influence, recognition and joy all flow from creating.

MAXIM 3: INCOME FOLLOWS ASSETS

Your job each year is to create new assets. An asset is anything that would still be valuable if you were hit by a bus.

Using this definition, it's easy to see why a house or shares are assets. If you were hit by a bus, your house and your shares wouldn't change in value.

In business it's exactly the same. Your business needs to be built so that it would still be valuable if you disappeared.

To do this, you need intellectual property assets. You must develop systems, methods and procedures. You need a brand and a culture. You need a system of marketing and selling your products and services.

When your business is in a position to carry on without you, then you have built yourself a whopping big asset.

You don't need to be overwhelmed by this concept. It takes time to build a whole business that can continue on without you. However, you can chip away at it each year.

Create documents. Every year create more and more of them. Sales scripts, training manuals, brochures, reports, checklists and best-practices.

Put them in writing, get a graphic designer to make them look pretty, then make sure they get used.

It seems challenging at first. However, pretty soon, you can't imagine running a business without them.

My mentor gave me this advice when I was really struggling. I had been through a tough year and had considered selling my business for £300k.

My mentor looked at my business and said "Income follows assets but you haven't built many."

Under my nose we discovered several great strategies that hadn't been documented. For a year, our team became driven to create documents and 12 months later the business was valued at £4m!

Maxim 4: Get known by the success of your clients

The best way to become famous is for what you have done for others.

If you focus on creating success for your clients, they will go out and tell the world. People are unlikely to believe what you say about yourself, but they will be very impressed by the favourable stories your clients are telling about you.

Most great businesses grow because of what others are saying about them. Google grew because people showed others how magical the results are when you "google" something. Facebook grew because of the sentence "are you on Facebook?" spoken between friends. Apple's meteoric growth in the 2000s was down to "raving Apple fans."

My own business success really took off when we focused centrally on the success of our clients as our business and marketing strategy.

As soon as people started hearing our client success stories, we had people beating down the door.

When it came time to invest in a social media campaign, we sent camera crews out to our clients' offices and let our clients tell their stories. As a result, we have dozens of video case studies that help us to generate all the business we can handle.

Rather than you beating the drum for yourself, beat the drum for your clients. Help them create a huge success story and then showcase it.

In many industries, if you genuinely do focus on the success of your clients, you will stand out like a beacon.

MAXIM 5: YOU ARE IN PARTNERSHIP WITH EVERYONE WHO TOUCHES YOUR BUSINESS

Seeing everyone who touches your business as a partner is a radical shift away from short-term, transactional behaviour towards long-term success for everyone.

See your team as partners, your suppliers as partners and even your customers as partners. Take the extra time to explore what success really looks like for everyone involved. Create deeper alignment in the needs and wants of everyone who's interacting with your business.

Don't see your business as an independent entity that can survive all on its own. See your business for what it is: a set of relationships that must last if success is to be achieved.

I'm not saying that you can never fire a poor-performing staff member or you can't end a supply deal on a product that isn't working out. Of course, any relationship can grow and evolve and it can also part ways when there's no longer alignment.

Transactional relationships are geared around getting the most out of an exchange in the immediate short term. The spirit of a good partnership is about working together to create success, now and in the future, for everyone involved.

Sometimes this means you can't take an immediate win in the short term and you have to look at the bigger picture.

When the recession hit, many big, cashed-up companies saw it as an opportunity to squeeze their suppliers and extend payment terms so they didn't have to pay suppliers for months after the invoice. In the short term they would definitely get a win by squeezing their suppliers for every drop but, in the long term, these suppliers begin to go bust, they look for ways to cut corners, they get sloppy and they simply can't produce their best work.

In some rare cases, big companies like the British retailer Waitrose worked closely with their suppliers to ensure they could ride out the recession and still produce good products. They found ways to support their long-term suppliers who were vulnerable to the financial crisis and, as a result, their suppliers found ways to help Waitrose. Their premium price brand has continued to expand despite the recession.

The spirit of partnership is a powerful driving force. It makes us think about the needs of others and work towards creating long-term success for everyone involved.

MAXIM 6: IDEAS ARE WORTHLESS, IMPLEMENTATION IS EVERYTHING

One of the most frustrating experiences of being well connected in the world of business is the constant question "What do you think of my idea?"

My response normally shocks people. I say "Ideas are worthless."

Anyone can sit around and have a big idea. Few can make it brilliant.

Let me give you two examples to illustrate my point.

Most Londoners love the experience of grabbing a sandwich from the UK fast-food sandwich giant, Pret A Manger. Pret stores are clean, the food is good, the service is friendly and you rarely have to wait too long in line. For that reason there are hundreds of Pret stores and the business is worth tens of millions of pounds.

Can you imagine the founders asking the question "We're going to make sandwiches; what do you think of our amazing idea?"

It's a dull idea. No one is going to get excited about a sandwich shop. Not until it's implemented with excellence. Even a boring idea becomes valuable when implemented insanely well.

In 2002, Bill Gates was telling people that the tablet PC would be the future of personal computing, so why isn't Microsoft the company famous for introducing us to these devices? They had the idea for tablet PCs in 2002; Steve Jobs didn't release the iPad until 2010!

Microsoft didn't implement the idea beyond its prototype. They waited around to watch Apple conduct the world's most successful product launch. Apple implemented the launch of this product so perfectly that they control the market for tablet PCs, and no one seems to be able to catch them.

In the example of Pret, a boring idea, beautifully implemented, became a hugely successful business. In the case of Microsoft's tablet PC, a brilliant idea, poorly executed, created no real value at all.

The value is in implementation. It's one thing to know that an Ascending Transaction Model would be good for your business, but it's a dedication to excellent implementation that will produce the results.

Maxim 7: Being imaginative is not being creative

Having an idea is easy. Creating something is difficult. Creating something takes focus, discipline and dedication.

If I told you I had created a cake, would you expect to be able to eat the cake?

Of course you would, because the word created literally means "to bring something into being; to cause something to become real in the world; to make something happen."

It does not mean "to have an idea, to think up something or to think about how something might happen."

Therefore, if I told you I "created" a cake, you have every right to expect to have a slice.

The word "creative" used to refer to the power to get something done. In some circles, however, it's come to mean "possessing the power to think things up."

Regularly, I hear people say to me "My problem is I never finish things because I'm too creative."

I've also had people say to me "I'm not very creative, but I'm very good at getting things done."

This tells me we have lost our way when it comes to understanding what it means to be "creative."

We've bought into the myth that what's going on in someone's head has value in the real world; it doesn't.

Thinking about murdering someone doesn't make you a murderer. Thinking about having a date with Pippa Middleton doesn't make you her new boyfriend.

Thinking about a business idea, a product or a new service doesn't make you its "creator."

What makes you creative is your ability to bring it into the world in a way that other people can understand and value.

As long as it's in your head, you haven't created anything yet. You *must* get it out into the real world in a way that shows up as valuable.

We need to use the word "imaginative" for people who have a lot of ideas. Imaginative people love to dream things up but the word does not imply they have brought their ideas into the world.

Being creative isn't easy; you need to decide upon the idea and then do everything required to bring it into the world. The process can take months or years to get a single creation completed. It's blood, sweat, tears, risk and sacrifice.

We should separate the dreamers from the doers and give more credit to the people who are truly creating things into existence.

To see Daniel talk about these maxims for high performance visit:

www.entrevo.com/talk-maxims

CHAPTER 13

THE VALUE CREATION CYCLE

You now have seven maxims that create a culture of high performance. You understand that you need to stretch, you are willing to get resourceful and be held accountable for the results.

Next we need a better understanding of how things move from ideas into valuable products or valuable businesses.

In this chapter we will take a look at how this happens so, every time you begin work on an idea, you know what lies ahead of you.

There's a predictable cycle that turns ideas into remarkably valuable creations.

You start out as imaginative, coming up with ideas that could work and you end up creating valuable products and businesses that make supernormal profits.

The journey along the way is entirely predictable:

1. **The idea.** The idea needs to be good and you need to turn your idea into a powerful pitch. However, as I said, there's no money in the ideas anymore. If you're waiting

for someone to come and write you a big fat cheque for your ideas, you're going to be waiting an awful long time. People don't pay for ideas, they pay for remarkable implementation; and you're a long way from that at the ideas stage.

2. **The mess.** As soon as you act upon your idea, you'll predictably make a mess. Having the idea that you want to bake a cake is easy, the next step is to find the ingredients and start baking. This takes time, energy and resources. If you start something and don't push through to completion all you do is make a mess. The disciplined creator doesn't start projects unless they are prepared to push through to a remarkable result. This is still quite far off if you're in the mess.

3. **The beta version.** When you begin working on your idea, only you truly understand what you're aiming for. Even when people give you feedback on your idea, you can't be sure that what's in their head is even remotely similar to what's in your head. Often people think they are on the same page when, in reality, they are worlds apart. Your first step, before you can get valuable feedback, is to create a beta version of your product or business. You should do this as quickly and cheaply as possible so, if the feedback is bad, you can change it easily and without being too discouraged. A beta product could actually be a well-designed brochure that features mock-up designs. It could be illustrations. It could be a competitor's product that's been altered for the purposes of illustrating your points of difference. The key here is to create something

that people can look at, touch, feel, listen to or experience in order for them to give you genuine insights based on a shared reality of your idea.

4. **The commercial version.** When you take on board the feedback you get from others, and the feedback you get from yourself once the beta version is complete, you will eventually make something that is ready to sell. A product or a service that others will pay for is what I call a commercial version. The commercial version is ready to go out and sell day to day. People will consider it against other commercial products or services and some people will then pay a normal price for your version. Predictably, a commercial version will generate enough money to cover your time in selling and producing it. This will often feel very disappointing after all the effort and money you've put in until now. I regularly see people who've spent over a year starting up a business get very discouraged when they start making an equivalent of their previous wage. Originally, they had imagined that this product, service or business was going to make a lot of money or provide a lot of freedom. Now it turns out that all the blood, sweat and tears that went into creating something merely pays a wage – and it requires work too! At this point, many people believe their idea is flawed and so they go back to the drawing board and have a completely new idea. This begins the cycle again. People who "make it" don't do this. Instead, they push through to the next step and build something that stands out as valuable.

5. **The remarkable version.** A remarkable product, service or business is one that people start to tell their friends about. It does something different, it's fresh, it's unique and it's valuable. Because people are talking about it, you get inbound enquiries, you make easier sales, you seem to be in demand and often you can charge a higher price. When you had a commercial version, it felt as if it was all about trading your time for money. Now you feel like you've created an asset! The energy required to take a commercial version to a remarkable version is often more than all the energy that went into creating a commercial version. The commercial version got you into the market, but the remarkable version is what everyone in the market wants to create. In order to build something remarkable, you have to take risks. You have to be willing to do things differently, you need to let your philosophy shine through and be willing to lose a few people because of it. To be remarkable, you need to invest in every touchpoint that exists in your business and make sure each and every step is worth talking about. A remarkable business has remarkable brochures, a remarkable sales process, a remarkable service process, a remarkable design, remarkable team members, a remarkable website ... and the list goes on. In the growth accelerator my company runs, we recommend to our clients that they make a list of every possible way a client "touches" their business and audit it. Ask the question: "Is this part of my business an idea, a mess, a beta version, a commercial version or is it remarkable?"

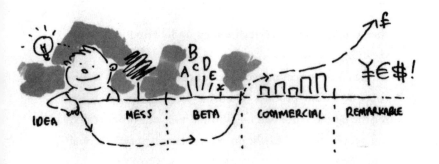

A profitable, growing business typically has a list of over 50% of all touchpoints in the business being remarkable.

THE FORMULA FOR MAKING SOMETHING REMARKABLE

There are three consistent ingredients I see, again and again, in remarkable businesses and products that people are driven to buy regardless of price.

1. IT MUST BE MEANINGFUL

Your buyers want products that matter. They want to buy things that have a story, that touch them emotionally. They want things that take them on a journey and that expand their world. They want to intertwine their own story with the products they buy. When Apple releases a new piece of video editing software they don't tell you about the software, they tell you about a group of friends who want to capture the memories of an important holiday. They want to make special videos to share with each other and never forget how fun the trip was. Steve Jobs was the master at taking the complex world of technology and presenting it in a meaningful way.

The key to making your product meaningful is to discover how your product or business changes people's lives for the better. Once you know what it is your product does for people, focus heavily on telling those stories through every interaction.

2. IT MUST BE DE-COMMODITIZED

Your creation can't be the same as everything else. A commodity sells for the lowest price; you can't afford to let your product or service be seen as just another version of the same thing. Commodities are easy to compare, de-commoditized products aren't.

The market won't pay much for salt, but it will pay a lot for "Himalayan Fairtrade Organic Mineral Rock Salt." Himalayan salt is special, you can't easily compare it to regular table salt and so it sells for ten times the price of table salt. Once again, we can learn from Apple Corporation; they created an operating system completely unique to them. Rather than turn their software into a commodity, where the market didn't value it, they created something that people couldn't easily compare to their PC rivals.

The key to de-commoditizing your creation is to develop your own philosophy. What won't you stand for? What are your design principles? What are you opposed to in your industry? What drives you?

All of these questions are based upon your philosophy. You must tune into your philosophy and then share it with everyone who comes in contact with your business.

Not everyone buys into the "organic" or "Fairtrade" philosophy. However, those people who do become very loyal to the brands that share their beliefs.

3. IT MUST BE OVER-SUBSCRIBED

Many business owners wrongly believe they can deliver value to the whole market and they set about trying to please everyone. The truth is, your business has limited capacity to take on clients and deal with them in a remarkable way. You need to know how many customers you can handle and then get "over-subscribed" for that number.

You must make sure you do not release your products in such a way that you end up with more products available than people who want to buy them. You need to release products only when there are ten times more people who've shown interest in them than what you have available. I use the 10 × rule when we are releasing a product. If I want to sell 50 products, I make sure we have 500 expressions of interest before we release it.

This process of becoming over-subscribed first requires you to know how many products you can deliver in a remarkable way. Then you must go out to market with the intent to have ten times that number of people "queuing up" to get one.

In the early days, this means you might be able to take on three clients per month, so you go out to get 30 people who are willing to complete a pre-client questionnaire. From the 30, you can select the three you most want to work with.

When you get these three ingredients right, your commercial version products will become remarkable. People will talk about them, buy them and enjoy them. Your business will stand out and you will thrive in the Entrepreneur Revolution.

To see Daniel talk about the value creation cycle visit:
www.entrevo.com/talk-value-cycle

CHAPTER 14

CREATE VS. CONSUME

When I share these predictable steps for creating something remarkable, some people get discouraged. They feel that it's going to be a long and difficult road ahead to build a profitable business, or a hot product or service.

While the idea of building every part of a business in a remarkable way feels heavy and daunting from the outset, the experience of actually doing it isn't.

The experience of building something that gets talked about is often the most rewarding and energetically uplifting thing you'll ever do.

Better yet, the results of having a remarkable business can be staggering. You don't just make wages, you make profits. You don't just help your clients, you blow their minds and make a difference to their lives! You don't just get a pat on the back, you get people raving about you!

There's little joy in the endless cycle of trying to come up with the "easy money-making idea." There's loads of joy in pushing something to be truly a stand-out.

Everything you consume requires energy – either to digest it, or to maintain it in your life.

Creating is opposite. When you create, energy flows through you. The act of creating wakes you up and makes you feel joyous.

If you don't believe me, go and look at the Forbes Rich List of self-made billionaires. Hardly any of them are retired. Almost none of them have used their wealth to lean back from life and sit on a beach endlessly consuming stuff. Most of them are typically engaged in the joy of creating, not the burden of consuming.

Steve Jobs was diagnosed with cancer but chose to spend his final years pouring himself into the act of creating. He could have chosen to do literally anything. No one would have judged him harshly if he chose to retire. Why did he stay in the game? Because creating is joyous. Leaning in is joyful.

Contrast Steve Jobs to the majority of lotto winners. It's a widely known statistical fact that most lotto winners become depressed and unhappy. They suddenly have the power to rapidly consume everything they ever dreamed of; and it sucks the life out of them.

For starters, the mere fact that they bought a lotto ticket shows you they were leaning back on life, looking for an exit. They then get the money and they go out to consume. Everything they buy comes with obligations to maintain it or digest it. It's exhausting and there's no joy in it.

Many people have fond memories of their college years. They were broke, they hardly owned a stick of furniture, they had to forage for money from under the sofa just to buy lunch, but they still remember this as a great time in their life. The reason people loved their college years was because they weren't weighed down with stuff, they were busy creating all the time and they didn't have the means to consume.

College, for most people, was a time when they had to invent their identity but, for some reason, people stop.

Keep doing it, keep reinventing yourself, keep creating.

CREATE THE FUTURE, DON'T CONSUME THE PAST

Don't fantasize about going back to the past as there's simply no such thing as "going back to the way things were." Life doesn't move backwards, it moves forward. There's no time machine coming to pick you up. You are not going back to your college years, the great year you had in 2003, or the good old pre-recession days. You are moving forward in time and the only way things will be better is if you create them as better.

Let me share a typical example of what happens when you try to go back in time. I once spontaneously went on an amazing holiday with friends to a place we'd never been before.

Without much planning we had to invent the trip as we travelled and we created the experiences on the go. We discovered unique places, we found ourselves in surprising and humorous situations, we met interesting people we didn't expect to meet. It turned out to be amazing and, the following year, we tried to do it again by going back to the same place and attempting to do the same things.

create!   consume!

When we got there it was not as fun. We tried to recreate "spontaneously meeting those hilarious people" and they weren't there. We attempted to revisit that "magical spot where everything just clicked" and it just didn't click.

It never works out trying to "get back" to the past; you can't do it.

Why didn't it happen? Because we were approaching the experience as a consumer. We were trying to consume an experience of the past rather than create something right now.

Let go of consuming the past. Let go of trying to "get back" to any place.

If you want more joy, stop consuming. Stop consuming people, things or events and stop trying to "get back" the past. Start creating the future. Reinvent yourself constantly, based on who you want to be.

CONSUMING IS A DRAIN, CREATING IS JOY

Now let's apply this to everyday life. It's time to stop reading books and write your own book. Stop attending events, plan your own event. Stop reading the news, start creating something newsworthy. Don't go looking for answers, start answering questions for others. Stop buying products, start creating your own products to deliver to the world.

Stop waiting for the right time, start creating the space for magic to happen.

When you replace your entire day with acts of creation, you will have energy. When you fill your day with acts of consumption you will burn out.

CHAPTER 15

LIVING THE DREAM

This final chapter is about making the final big change that will allow you to live the dream and enjoy the great opportunities of the Entrepreneur Revolution.

In the Industrial Revolution, humans were seen to be part of the machinery. The system was designed to dehumanize workers, to get them to tune out from their inner calling and to get on with whatever tasks they had been assigned.

As a result, many people forgot what it was to be human. In the western world, we detuned from our humanity to such a great extent that it's probably no coincidence that epidemics of depression have affected millions of people.

A big part of the Entrepreneur Revolution is rediscovering your humanity. At the core of the Entrepreneur Revolution is love.

Let's discuss why the Entrepreneur Revolution is powered by it.

This may sound very soppy and unbusinesslike, but nothing could be further from the truth. It's actually very logical, practical and real. If love is missing from your business, your business will not survive in the future.

You must love what you do, your team must love working in your business, your clients must love buying from you and your community must love having your business within it.

To explore how massive this trend is, let's go back in time.

THE AGE OF "HANDS"

For thousands of years, humanity thrived because of our hands. Humans developed dexterity and we became brilliant tool makers.

We could precisely move objects in such a way that we could shape the world to our will.

We made weapons that could take down a mighty wildebeest. We made ploughs that could turn a dry patch of land into a fertile crop. We developed looms that could make warm cloths and shield us from the elements.

The most admired men in society were those who were strong with their arms and precise with their aim. Kings were judged on their prowess with a sword and leaders were elected because of their skills in battle.

No other animal on earth could compete with our ability to move objects so precisely and we became the most dominant species on earth as a result.

In the 1500s, the Renaissance celebrated human dexterity by producing fine art. Our precision had evolved to a point that Michelangelo fashioned the mighty David from stone, with his gaze mesmerizing and his form considered perfect.

The "age of hands" took us right up until the dawn of the Industrial Revolution when something very strange happened: we created machines that could beat us at our own game.

THE AGE OF "HEADS"

The machines we built in the Industrial Revolution superseded our own dexterity. One industrial sewing machine could outperform one hundred fine tailors, one tractor could outperform one hundred diligent farmers, one engine could outperform one hundred strong men working a pulley.

What happened, as a result, was a huge displacement of workers. Unemployment went through the roof as technology removed the need for thousands of well-trained hands.

Then came the thinking men. Carnegie, with his ingenious Bessemer Steel Process; Rockefeller with his standardized distribution model for oil; JP Morgan with his financial weapons of mass acquisition; Onassis with his new type of oil tankers.

Suddenly, the most powerful men on earth were not particularly talented with their hands, they were brilliant with their minds. They could out-think their opponents.

First came the strategists. Rockefeller rethought the way oil was distributed. Carnegie rethought the steel-making process. Morgan rethought financial products. Onassis rethought the way oil was shipped internationally.

Then came the second round big thinkers. Along came Sam Walton with his Wal-Mart megastores, Ingvar Kamprad with his IKEA furniture, Bill Gates with his Microsoft operating systems and Larry Ellison with his Oracle databases.

The age of heads meant the highest-paid people on earth were thinkers. Lawyers, accountants, scientists, company directors, managers and CEOs became the leaders in our society.

The age of heads – or the "information age," or the "ideas economy" – produced wild new innovations that transformed humanity and humanity's place in the world.

Then, once more, something strange happened. We built machines that could beat us at our own game for a second time: we created computers.

The "age of heads" took us right up until the dawn of the Entrepreneur Revolution (now) when something very strange happened again.

THE AGE OF "HEARTS"

One piece of software could do the work of one hundred accountants, one website could do the work of one hundred managers, one automated system could outperform one hundred scientists.

Just as machines became better than us at dexterity, computers are now better than us at thinking.

A new type of technology took over, the technology of intimacy.

Intimacy is about knowing what someone else is experiencing. It's about knowing what you are thinking, what you are feeling, what you've seen, what you've heard, what you've tasted and smelled. It's about knowing who you are friends with, who you like, what you like and what interests you. It's about sharing – everything.

Does that sound familiar? It should – it's the biggest business in town now.

Social networks and social media were born as a way to share our experiences of life.

Through the act of sharing and caring and liking and discussing we've seen multi-billion dollar businesses created in just a few short years.

It's not just the Mark Zuckerbergs of the world who are making money. All over the world, people are running their small businesses and discovering the effect of using social media and social networks.

If you care about your clients, listen to them, talk to them and share experiences with them. Treat them like you would treat a friend and you will find your business is booming.

This is why I say the new game is love.

The companies that will do well in the future are the ones that discuss love in the boardroom.

They will ask questions such as:

"How would we build this business in a way that people love working with us, love shopping with us, love supplying us, love talking about us and love to see us doing well?"

Talking about growing sales, beating the competition and dominating the market will not get any of those things achieved. Talking about "love" will.

Love is about passion, love is about care, love is about intimacy, love is about ... love.

Starbucks will do well if it continues to love creating the best coffee experience. Apple will do well if it continues to love creating the world's best consumer technology. BP will come back if it decides to love powering the planet in a way that makes sense for everyone now and in the future.

Once again there are going to be tough times ahead as people make this change.

Countless men were put out of work because their hands were no longer needed and their heads were not trained for the ideas economy. Likewise, countless people will be put out of work because their heads are no longer needed and their hearts haven't been trained for the entrepreneur economy.

Just like "hands people" would have rejected the concept of a "thinking economy," we will see many "heads people" rejecting the concept of a "loving economy."

Just as there was turbulence during the transition into the industrial economy, there will be turbulence as we transition into the entrepreneurship economy.

The good news is that you now know what you have to do, and I think you will like it because your job in the *new* economy is to love what you do.

All of the doing innovation has been done for you in the form of low-cost manufacturing and distribution options. All the thinking innovation has been done for you in the form of readily available software solutions. All that is left for you to do is to come into your industry with more love than anyone else.

You need to care about the customer experience (which might even start by calling them something other than a "customer"). You need to become more connected with what people in your industry are thinking and feeling. You must learn to talk openly about why others might love being part of your vision.

The pay-off is huge. Can you imagine waking up every day and getting paid to do what you love? Can you imagine hearing back from people who say you delivered real value to them and, because of that, they simply love to do business with you?

Can you imagine living in the entrepreneur sweet spot?

1. You do what you are passionate about.
2. You deliver amazing value.
3. You get paid well for it.

… and everyone loves you for it.

For the first time in history this isn't just a dream for a few, it's a reality for millions.

Money won't make you happy, being skilled won't make you happy, knowing your passion won't make you happy.

Combining all three of these things will leave you feeling over the moon!

I live my life in this sweet spot. It blows my mind some days just how lucky I am. I travel, I earn amazing money and my clients report back to me that they love doing business with us.

I want you to know that if you aren't quite there yet, keep leaning in. Keep going. The juice *is* worth the squeeze. It's going to be worth it. You're going to make it. You're living in the most amazing time to be alive and you're reading this book for a reason.

I want to encourage you to re-read this book a few times. Some of the ideas hit you the second time around. I know I cover topics quickly and jump from idea to idea. In the second or third read, you will spot something magical. You will click an idea into place and it might just take everything up a notch.

For whatever reason, you were born into these times. You could have been born any other time in history and your battle would have been with disease, hunger or conflict.

Any other time in history and you wouldn't have had a voice or a platform to share your message. Any other time in history and your ideas would live and die in your head without seeing the light of day.

Who knows why, but here you are living in a time when anything is possible, where you do have a voice, where your ideas can come to life and where you can empower yourself and others through enterprise.

You're here in the right time and the right place in history to make a difference and to live out your own fairytale.

Don't waste a day. These revolutionary times don't come around often. Seize this day today as your moment. Put down this book and become the person you dreamed you would be.

Let the world be your playground as you embrace your role in the Entrepreneur Revolution.

READ THIS BOOK MORE THAN ONCE

This book contains some powerful ideas. I believe now you're at the end of this book you're ready to perform at a whole new level.

Did you keep an eye out for the new ingredient that must go into everything you do?

I mentioned this ingredient many times in the book but I couldn't say what it is specifically for you. I will leave you to find it.

When you read through this book, did you look for the clues?

The beginning was important, the end is significant but at the centre is where you might find you discover a mountain of value you never noticed when you first looked.

Sometimes people read this book and "get it"; other times they don't. Some people "get it" on the second or third read. I've not hidden this key ingredient from you – if anything it's actually right under your nose.

Whatever you do, don't stop looking. You simply can't build a successful enterprise without this ingredient in the Entrepreneur Revolution.

CASE STUDIES OF "ENTREPRENEUR REVOLUTIONARIES"

Adèle Thèron

Adèle loves change. Not in the way most people do, as in a holiday or a new outfit. She loves change as a concept; she loves the process of radical transformation.

This love led her to work for several large consulting companies, getting paid megabucks to help large teams of people move on from the shock associated with clashes during mergers, outsourcing or downsizing projects, so they are focused on moving on versus being held back.

Within this corporate sphere, she developed a method for helping people to rapidly transform their lives even after a major setback or turbulent event.

She loved helping people to change and transform but she got frustrated with the structure of the corporate environment.

She felt large companies were missing the humanity of what she was doing. Rather than seeing the radical nature of what's possible for people who go through a changing time, she was being asked to simply tick the boxes in implementing change programmes which were mostly about delivering KPIs vs. checking that everyone is emotionally on board.

She decided to set about the task of taking radical transformation to the world. She chose a niche that was close to her heart, helping women who have been through a divorce to recreate their life.

Adèle named her process "the naked divorce." She wrote a book on the topic, created products and found partners. She started speaking publicly and soon became a recognized key person of influence in the field.

She constructed an Ascending Transaction Model of products that could be shipped internationally. Soon her business started to attract clients all over the world and partnerships in countries she'd never been to.

She's free to travel, explore and develop herself and her business.

Today she runs a successful global small business and helps men and women all over the world to heal from their divorce. She's taking her methodology and using it to create programmes for other types of emotional trauma. She's still able to consult for corporations and, with her new-found passion, she is able to charge more and do work on her terms.

Adèle let go of the normal corporate work ethos and embraced her passion. She's turned her passion into a business, she delivers massive value and gets well rewarded for it. Adèle is doing what she loves and is already living in the Entrepreneur Revolution.

Jeremy Harbour

Jeremy loves deals. He dropped out of school at age 15 to buy and sell goods at a local market. By 18 he'd built a local amusement arcade but, by 20, he went bust and had to start from scratch again.

He did a deal and got started in a telecommunications company. He did some customer deals and it grew. He did lots more deals and he built a large database of clients. He did a partnership deal with a UK membership organization and ended up with a national business before the age of 30.

At age 34 he did an exit deal and sold his business for a lot of money.

After that he had no reason to work unless he was doing what he loved; which boils down to doing deals.

Today Jeremy lives in the Balearic Islands. He advises people on doing deals all over the world.

On a typical day he will be sitting on his balcony in the sun overlooking a gorgeous Mediterranean bay with his headset on. He uses Skype to advise people on their deals. He helps people buy businesses for the best price, he helps turn around businesses that are in distress, he helps people sell their businesses for a lot of money.

Rather than taking fees, he takes a percentage of the deal. He makes a small fortune each year based on the success of his deals.

His set-up allows him to travel for about five months of the year without missing a thing. He "works" a few hours each day from anywhere in the world. In his spare time, he's been able to write a book, give talks at conferences and he's even setting up an art studio to explore any hidden talent he might have for sculpture.

Jeremy isn't stuck in a small business like many people are. He's well aware of the exciting times we live in and he's making the most of it. He's turned his passion for deal making into an exciting business. He's doing what he loves and he's already living in the Entrepreneur Revolution.

SHÁÁ WASMUND

Sháá loves partnerships. Her whole career was about putting together strategic alliances and partnership deals. She did this for some of the best brands and high-profile people in the world.

Eventually, Sháá decided it was time to do this for herself and she launched her business Smarta, a website that helps small businesses to grow.

In the first year of her business, tragedy struck and she became a widow and a single mother.

Determined not to go back into employment, she went out to create strategic partnerships that would benefit her business, her clients and her partners. She aligned her business to big businesses, to celebrities and to well-known brands.

She worked with her partners to create a bundle of resources and products that every small business needs. Today, over 350,000 small businesses a month use her business to grow.

Sháá has gone on to create a national awards programme for her clients, she has become a best-selling author and she's able to work from home most days too! Sháá is doing what she loves and is already living in the Entrepreneur Revolution.

JACQUI SHARPLES

Jacqui loves fitness. On most nights of the week you can find her at the athletics field, pole vaulting or sprinting. She believes fitness is what gives people their spark.

Nothing could have illustrated this more than when Jacqui left her corporate job. After years as an engineer in a construction firm she realized that a lot of her colleagues were losing their fitness and losing their will to live.

In a bold move, she quit her high-paying job and got trained up as a fitness trainer. She began delivering fitness training sessions before work in the parks in Melbourne.

After the business started moving, she decided to hone in on a niche and focus her efforts exclusively on corporate women in their 30s.

Jacqui has written a book, created an ATM of products and is now expanding her business with other trainers who want to use her system. In a short space of time, she's become a key person of influence in her field.

She created a specialized programme called "Love Your Body, Love Your Life" that includes elements of fitness and life coaching to help her clients get fit and reclaim their spark.

She's replaced her high-paid engineering income and now engineers spectacular transformations for her clients along with constructing the life she wants. Jacqui is doing what she loves and is already living in the Entrepreneur Revolution.

MIKE SYMES

Mike Symes loves brands. Not just any brands, he loves financial brands like credit cards, banks, investment funds and insurance.

In his career at a US bank he worked his way up to the head marketing role. Within his role he ticked all the boxes, won several awards and then decided he'd be happier running his own business.

He left his high-paying job with hundreds of people on his team to start a two-person operation with no offices. At first it must have been both thrilling and scary to give up on the high-flying career, but Mike knew he could create something special if he stuck with it.

Today, Mike runs a financial branding business in London and New York. He's the author of a book and has developed an ATM of products that serve his clients and take them on a journey.

He has developed his own special method for "igniting a brand, illuminating its points of difference and making its messages spread like wildfire." Now it's his clients who are winning awards!

Mike is busy and he loves it. He's building a fast-growth global small business and his clients just can't get enough of it. He's regularly featured in his industry press, his book keeps selling and he speaks all over the world. Mike is doing what he loves and is already living in the Entrepreneur Revolution.

To see video of these and other case studies visit:

www.entrevo.com/case-studies

ACKNOWLEDGEMENTS

The ideas in this book have come about from many wonderful conversations with important people in my life over the last 15 years.

I would like to sincerely thank:

My parents Andrew and Diane for fostering my entrepreneurial spirit, always encouraging my ideas as well as offering practical support.

My sister Justine for her spark and enthusiasm and friendship.

Aléna Dundas who consistently brings out the best in me.

My best mates and business partners Marcus Ubl and Glen Carlson. Long may our adventures continue.

Vac Ubl: as a newbie you seemed to spoil a lot of good ideas with sobering advice but, strangely, the older I get the wiser you got.

My business mentors who have taken me under their wing over the last 15 years (Jon, Roger and others), especially in the last few years Mike Harris who has been the most amazing mentor a guy could ask for.

The mentor teams on the "Key Person of Influence Program" – Mike Harris, Darren Shirlaw, Mindy Gibbons-Klein, Nic Rixon, Penny and Thomas Power, Sháá Wasmund, Steve Bolton, Ian Elliot, Andrew Griffiths, Marc Johnstone, Kylie Bartlett and Cathy Burke.

Some great entrepreneurial friends who have stimulated my thinking – Jeremy Harbour, Oli Barret, Tom Ball, Julia Langkraehr, Jeremy Jauncy, Keiron Sparrowhawke, Lara Morgan, Paul Dunn, Callum Laing and Margaret Loh.

To the awesome people on our team who are building daily the most dynamic, high-performance entrepreneurial ecosystem.

To the investors in my businesses who have joined me in taking the financial risks required to power up a big vision.

To my awesome clients who teach me so much about the entrepreneurial journey and who keep my spark burning for an unfolding Entrepreneur Revolution.

ABOUT DANIEL PRIESTLEY

Daniel Priestley is a successful entrepreneur, international speaker and best-selling author. Daniel started out as an entrepreneur in 2002 (at age 21) and built a multi-million-dollar event marketing and management business before age 25. He has since built several successful businesses in the UK, Australia and Singapore.

Daniel has bought, sold and turned around businesses in his career as an entrepreneur. He has raised money and built businesses in multiple countries. He's fortunate to be mentored by Mike Harris who has built three iconic, multi-billion-pound businesses.

Daniel Priestley has raised hundreds of thousands of pounds for charity and served on the board for several organizations. He's a best-selling author and international speaker.

In 2010, Daniel launched an entrepreneur growth accelerator designed to assist in supporting small businesses through a growth phase. Each year, in several cities around the world, Daniel's team selects small businesses to go through this nine-month growth process. The accelerator programme has attracted the support of highly celebrated business leaders, investors and companies.

Daniel is known for coining the phrase "global small business" and has been sharing the concept of an "Entrepreneur Revolution" since 2007.

You can keep in touch with Daniel on his blog: www.entrevo.com/blog or on Twitter: www.twitter.com/danielpriestley.

WHAT NEXT?

After reading this book you might feel inspired to learn more, keep in touch and meet other entrepreneurial revolutionaries.

Daniel Priestley's company Entrevo regularly hosts events, webinars, discussions, pitching competitions and networking (online and in the "real world").

To see what's coming up visit www.entrevo.com.

BONUS: If you would like to review this book, we will reward you for taking the time to do so. Here's how:

1 Write a review of this book.
2 Post it on Amazon, iTunes Bookstore, your blog, your Facebook page, or get it published in another publication.
3 Send a link or a screenshot to reviews@entrevo.com.
4 You will be sent free tickets to upcoming events or receive samples of new products and services from Entrevo (depending on where you are and what we have going on at the time).